The Untold Story
of
the Karbon Baby

Heru Hainus

D1114150

The Untold Story of Karbon Baby
Heru Hainus
Copyright © 2021 Heru Hainus

ISBN #: 9798546902032

Bible versions used in this book.

KJV—King James Version, public domain.

NIV—Holy Bible, New International Version®, NIV® Copyright ©1973, 1978, 1984, 2011 by Biblica, Inc.® Used by permission. All rights reserved worldwide.

CONTENTS

DEDICATION

Dedicated to Ziahnn Ziare Sykes,
besides air, my only other reason for breathing.

INTRODUCTION

Karbon Babies

If necessity is the mother of invention, then desperation must be the father that forces her to bare more children. If the addition of this adage possesses any shred of viability whatsoever, then there just may be hope for those who consider themselves to be heirs to the Most High's energy. Our position is one in which we must take back our earth by *all* means necessary and, fortunately for us, this spiritual coup d'état is in an atmosphere of desperation.

What does it matter if you have food for the mind and soul, when both lands are in the hands of your enemies? Does it not bother you that the harvest is plenty from both lands and yet the number one cause of death is starvation? This is why a pastor can preach until five loaves and three fish multiply to feed five thousand, yet as soon as the masses leave God's house, they are too ashamed to admit that they are still impoverished.

The same eventuality is mirrored on the physical plane, where people don't stop eating when their stomachs are full, rather they stop when the package is empty! This palpable illusion is what breeds the cyclic behavior where you eat only because it tastes good (physical plane) and you only listen/react (spiritual plane) because it sounds good, subsequently nurturing a realm that is fueled by greed and gluttony.

Our liberation rests on the paradigm crafted by Dr. Neely Fuller and expounded on by the great Dr. Frances Cress Welsing, stipulating that freedom must be achieved in *every area* of life activity, those of which are education, economics, entertainment, sex, law, politics, labor, religion, and *war*. Any measurable difference in any area aforementioned when crafting a cosmic reawakening seals one's demise.

If we think for ourselves in entertainment but not economics, how will that help us? If we think for ourselves in labor but not politics, again how will that help us? As you can see, when you juxtapose each area with each other and are able to spot highly noticeable disparities, you encroach upon an undesirable and immutable paradox, that *all* energy is connected, and that the compartmentalization of information is the smoke and mirrors of European sorcery.

Mother Earth desires a different story to be told, a more powerful and meaningful narrative to be written. She told you to revisit the Periodic Table of Elements, and right in plain sight you will bear witness to the beginning! If organic chemistry is the study of Carbon, then why is Carbon not residing all by itself? If it is the King of Elements, according to the so-called Europeans, why is it the same size as all the other elements? Is the king in chess the same size as the pawns?

We know that the so-called Europeans associate size with importance, so logic dictates if this was the "Table" that spoke their story, and if Carbon was a significant part of their physical makeup, the King of Elements would have been immortalized as the key to what makes "whiteness" great. It would have been the justification they would have used to subjugate the "less-evolved races" because we know, even without this being the case, that Western civilization has always used its "science" to accommodate this construct.

All you need to do is look at the maps, where Europe and North America are the same size as Africa, when nearly four US land masses can fit inside the Motherland! Yes, the Most High said to revisit the "Table," so you can eat and fill yourself and eliminate hunger among your people.

As you can sense, I make no apologies when referring to the Most High as a dominant female energy! I do so without any reservations, for I have awakened from the despotic rule of a patrilineal society. If there is any doubt in you, when exposed to the "Table," I am sure that your ambivalence will be short-lived. For those who are adept we know that the Most High is *both* forms of energy, male and female, *just like you*! The difference lies in the ratio of male/female energy.

A woman produces estrogen and testosterone, does she not? But her energy still leans more toward femininity. A man also produces estrogen and testosterone, which is imperative for healthy sexual growth and function, but his energy still leans toward masculinity, does it not? I make no apologies as well for framing this reason through a traditional lens regarding masculinity and femininity. This duality exists in us all, but it is the ratio of male to female energy, along with other peculiarities, that makes us who we are.

Those who are adept, also are aware of "as above, so below." The male Y chromosome is one third the size of the X chromosome as the Blanco "science" states, the X containing somewhere around 900 genes in contrast to 55 genes for the Y.

I will also make no apologies for asserting that there is no such thing as Blanco "science," just *our* religion masquerading as their science dressed in the hideous garb we acknowledge as the English language. You refer to your planet as Mother Earth, your land as the Motherland, and your nurturer as Mother Nature. A woman's energy outnumbers a man's energy in terms of population *globally*!

Black people say that we are a spiritual people, but if we were to be brutally honest, we would have to confess, as Black men, that there is *no one* on this planet more spiritual than Black women. Regardless of outlook and spiritual background, it is usually the Black woman who introduces the Black man to the commitment of spiritual guidance, the evidence can be easily seen in any church in Black neighborhoods.

The energy from the Most High flowing through the veins of our superwomen is what has contributed most to manifesting this reality. They adulterate, then dominate the energy to ensure we remain disconnected. Why do you think in European society that propaganda can make Black women appear unattractive, due to their skin tone, but in the same breath make the male with the same skin tone attractive? If the woman is powerless in European culture, why does the man have to attain power just to have her?

The purpose of this new narrative is not just to wake you, but to keep you out of the bed so you do not fall back asleep! The Metu Neter has called on her warriors to cast away any doubt, to shed skin he told you was made of dust. It is time for the Black/real superman and superwoman to reunite, reinforcing and fostering each other's strength that was made anew by recapturing and redirecting the energy in every area of life activity.

From this union, the Black superwoman in nine months will invite the Most High's spirit as an honored guest at her "Table" and the Most High shall appear in the form resembling the delicate hands of a midwife, there to help facilitate the greatest creation, and to replay the sounds of Nature's greatest masterpiece . . . the cries of the Karbon baby.

Heru Hainus

PART 1

Karbon Built the Matrix

The King of Elements is the title given to this cosmic energy, which is said by the so-called Europeans to have created the earth's universe. This energy is many, yet one, articulating itself as different manifestations of the same phenomenon. It is the food you eat, the buildings you live and work in, the air you breathe out, and the life blood of the so-called Europeans' transportation networks.

You know this elemental energy as Carbon, though it is worth noting that Carbon is only Latin for *coal*! It is even more important to know that just because you can name something does not mean that you know what it is, which subsequently, and unbeknownst to the Black conscious mind, feeds the Blanco's superiority complex while simultaneously leaving a chasm between you and the untapped potential of the Most High's power.

From here on in this book, you will hear me characterizing these beings as Blancos and not so-called Europeans, because those who are adept, and who are fully aware, know that they were not the first in Europe, as even their argument for racial evolution supports the aforementioned assertion. That argument being one in which they theorize that man migrated out of his home in Africa to other regions of the earth and gradually devolved in melanin potency (remember, we can't frame the outlook as if Blancos lost melanin because they still do possess a type of melanin).

We must also realize the reason for the disagreement is not in the common ground that has been established between Black truth and Blanco lies (that *all* people come from Africa). It is at what point in their evolution that they are willing to admit there was any contribution from our people essential for the existence, growth, and development of their race. As stated before, they have no problem saying humans trace their origins back to the Motherland; where their issue lies is when Black people try to claim credit for the growth and development of Blanco culture, (that is, the arts, sciences, and spiritual frameworks).

So, the real question would be, how long do Blancos claim eumelanin took to *devolve* into expressing pheomelanin? You have also probably wondered about the title of this book; the spelling of Carbon is changed to Karbon. The reason for this is for you to *always* associate the study of Carbon, which we know in their schools as "organic chemistry," as a discipline that reached its known apex in Khemit and not in the modern Western world or in modern Asia. So Karbon will be used from here on.

Last, but not least, let us not get caught up in going too deep in what the original names of many of these disciplines and territories were. We will go deep enough to bring the credit and its links *back to us,* not to mention there are many people who are unaware of the arcane expressions that characterized us and the places of long ago, but many are aware of the current terms.

Before you can convince someone of anything, you must first establish common ground. This is why I place quotation marks around terms frequently used by Blancos, which I think aids in encouraging this much-needed paradigm shift, and not the terms that may or may not be used by melanin-rich people in their conscious community.

You must always realize that without Karbon, life on this planet cannot and would not exist! Remember, that the best way to hide a poker hand is with a plain face, the best way to hide a gorgeous body is in plain clothes, and the *only* way to hide the answers to life's mysteries is in plain sight! How many of us have been in chemistry class only to be daydreaming about how we couldn't wait to become an adult so that we didn't have to come to these "useless" classes and get on with what's truly important, like becoming a rapper, a model, or a sports star, because of course the likelihood of these outcomes is high.

What we never chose to embrace is how crucial this discipline is in gaining a greater understanding of the world around us and, more important, a greater understanding of us as a people. $C_{18}H_{10}N_2O_4$ is a formula the Most High had to declare as a eureka moment, because it became the formula that allowed the doors to open, gaining access to the celestial body we know as the Sun, the central power source of radiation.

$C_{18}H_{10}N_2O_4$ is the formula for the melanin molecule. This is the formula that allows you access to what Blanco science characterizes as the electromagnetic spectrum. What is incredibly important about this formula, which is overlooked and marginalized, is that it is overlooked and marginalized by *us* and not the "scientific community!"

We as a people are the ones who have not truly realized and understood the importance of its chemical makeup, which in turn has led us to be confused about our position in this realm, enslaved by a language that emphasizes the importance of specificity, which is the key difference in one speaking with conviction, in contrast to sweeping generalities. How often have you heard people use Karbon and some say melanin, leaving the listener who is not well learned to assume they are completely unrelated?

Out of the thirty-four atom molecules they know as melanin, eighteen or, in other words, more than half is Karbon! You have to start looking at melanin as a supercharged form of Karbon! When you go back and look at that "Table," all will be known to you. When you are taught the basics of how the "Table" is set up, you begin to redefine and then recalibrate your energy to where it should be aligned, as determined by natural order or the Metu Neter and not by societal constructs.

That "Table" is *about you*! If the Bible is the manuscript that tells the story of our people in the *above*, then the "Periodic Table of Elements" is the manuscript that tells the story of what happened *below*. I will say it again, and with *conviction,* that our religion became their science, because you would be out of your mind to think that the Most High would tell you to "be fruitful and multiply" and essentially live life at an optimal level and not give you the secrets to do so.

As you know by now, if you have lived long enough, anything worth knowing has always started off as a secret first. The "colors" you see are part of the "visible spectrum" from the "electromagnetic spectrum" that is emitted from our central radiation source you know as the Sun. See, what most people don't know is that in their "schools" we are taught that the primary colors are blue, red, and yellow. That may be true for "material colors," but in the world of physics, which is the world of Khemistry, the primary colors are blue, red, and *green*.

See how in order to gain clarity in this matrix crafted by the Blancos, you only come closer to truth with specificity than you do with generalities, removing yourself from allowing terms and concepts to be used interchangeably. One must know that when mixing the primary colors in the world of physics—red, green, and blue—you get the color "white" and to get this color one must mix these primary colors evenly, then you shall get your desired "gray" or "white."

This is why the Blanco associates "white" with purity and everything that is holy and sacred, but yet "black" is the color that absorbs *all* light or all the primary colors giving back to the human eye a color that "appears black," because instead of reflecting light, it is absorbing it! White is the "color" we "see" when all the colors or wavelengths are being reflected! So, the question is, what is the life force behind *melanated beings* in that when the primary colors mix, there is more absorption rather than the giving off of energy? Because we know that "light" is just another euphemism for radiation, we are beings who possess a "color" that can absorb the Sun's energy and reimagine it in ways that will ironically justify the fears of the Blanco, elucidating why this very fear has plagued them since their conception.

"White" is also known as the "colorless color." If you were to make an effort to make a "white paint," you would have to use all sorts of different chemicals, most of them toxic, in order to get the color "white." So, in essence, the form of melanin they have is a shell, vessel, or *"skin,"* if you will, that is incapable of absorbing large amounts of radiation, hence the Blanco's inherent fear of radiation as well as a fear of those who can absorb it at a much higher level.

We accomplish such a herculean feat with a super-charged form of Karbon known as eumelanin. There are a few types of melanin: (eumelanin) the black/brown combination, (pheomelanin) the orange/red combination, (neuromelanin) the dark matter in the brain, (allomelanin), which is also a dark melanin that is found in fungi and has no nitrogen in its molecular formula, and (pyomelanin) also a black/brown combination found in bacteria.

It is also interesting to note that their "scientists" have found a link between pigmentation and bacterial pathogenicity, which basically means "color" has a lot to do with the evolution of an organism within its host. As usual, these are the simple things, adulterated with scientific jargon, that are remade into being of mysterious origin and convoluted so that the information is ignored, overlooked, or hard to understand.

We are all well aware when the body is suffering from an infection or a bruise. In that region there will be discoloration or the breaking of light to indicate that there has indeed been damage done to a vessel that was designed to *absorb* light, whether that be at the low end of the spectrum where Blancos exist, or the higher end of the spectrum where the black/brown combination maximizes its potential.

To complicate matters even further, the skin is not her-alded for its original purpose but merely as a covering, if you will, that houses all the important organs. Without the skin, the body's largest organ, it would be impossible for the important organs to survive; one would lose their physical identity, not to mention there would be no way to interact with the outside environment, as it serves as an interface, or the shared boundary between spirit and reality. We give so much attention to the brain but fail to realize that the brain gets much of its intel from the *skin*!

We have already concluded that we are equipped with a spiritual molecule that is likened to a supercharged form of Karbon, so we might as well start referring to our skin as a web of hypersensitive light-gathering molecules, that holds the potential to transform itself into anything that bonds in crystal formation, which is practically everything, because Karbon only bonds in a form called diamond cubic.

Let's not get too far ahead of ourselves just yet because many have a hard time believing that the skin is designed to absorb light, not only to put makeup and tattoos on. This is the only time I will admit that there may be some shred of truth that Black people may be too far gone, because we always had to prove that an institutional framework, built on lies, is lying. We have to cite their sources and receive approval from their committees before our work and projects can be validated and yet Trump and Gates can be newcomers in their respective fields, little to no experience whatsoever, and still become men of power, knowing that in their matrix, it is one thing to have an opinion but it is another thing to have an opinion in the position of authority.

So I think I can kill two birds with one stone in this instance. On one hand, it satisfies the scholarly mind as they seek as much information, regardless of the race of the person who is the resource, as well as comforting the mind of the Oreo who needs the Blanco to nod his head first before he can agree with what is written and spoken and already validated and codified by natural law.

To make a long story short, we about to quote some White folks. Nina G. Jablonski is a professor and head of the Department of Anthropology at Pennsylvania State University. In her book, titled *Skin: A Natural History,* she states,

"The size and shape of melanosomes [small membrane-bound packets where melanin is produced], as well as the way they aggregate, influence their ability to protect the skin and underlying tissues from UVR [ultraviolet radiation]. In darkly pigmented skin, the melanosomes are larger, melanin-rich, and dispersed evenly within keratinocytes. This arrangement permits them to absorb more energy than the smaller, less dense, and more lightly melanized melanosomes of lightly pigmented skin" (Jablonksi, 2006, 66).

She goes on to say something peculiar about this energy that we have already identified as a supercharged form of Karbon, stating,

"Melanocytes originate near the spinal cord in the developing embryo, at the neural crest, where they are known as melanoblasts. Early in the embryo's development, they migrate throughout the body to find their way into the skin, ears, brain, and eyes, where they produce pigment" (Jablonski, 2006, 67).

They are referred to as migratory cells, essentially colonizing the body so that the body or vessel can have the opportunity to experience light at its highest level! Let's entertain one more assertion from the Blanco scientist, which you have already gathered through empirical data, because you have the type of skin that absorbs the Sun in ways they have yet to duplicate naturally, only artificially. I love this quote because it gets straight to the point. "Some of the most important properties of skin are related to sunlight" (Jablonski, 2006, 10).

So, logic dictates if we possess a form of melanin that is larger in size, uniform in structure, and highly efficient in terms of light absorption, why does the discipline of politics say that our skin doesn't matter and that we should treat the skin as an invisible cloak until it indicates to us that we are now too old and life is nearing its end? This is facts over feelings; we are not here to imagine that we are all the same; we are here to acknowledge our differences and accept them because acceptance leads us being placed to rightful positions in the cosmological seating while simultaneously uncovering the real reason for the perpetual hatred levied against a people born with the gift.

How are you shouting we are the same when Nature has already stated that we are different? It is their society that gives difference a negative connotation, not Nature. The "dominant class" had to construct an image and a worldview, telling a biased story about the mysteries of life because Nature awaits, desperately eager to tell its own.

Again, we go back to the "Table" to garner clarity, when you look at the Periodic Table of Elements, there is a method to the madness, the elements are not placed in their positions by chance. From left to right, they go up in order by atomic mass (atomic mass is when you add the protons and neutrons together). The horizontal rows are called periods. The vertical rows are called groups or families, if you will, because they tend to exhibit the same "behavior."

The Karbon group is called Karbon14 because it is the fourteenth vertical row. The nickname for this group, which was given by Blancos, is the "crystallogens." You have to commit to memory that Karbon *only* bonds in a form called diamond cubic, which means it only bonds in cubes to create these crystals.

Diamond is an adjective and it is Greek for "invincible," because when the Greeks ran into the hardest substance on earth, that is how they sought to describe it. They have always tried to peer into the darkness of the cube, only to realize the misalignment with reality and spirit occurs because the vessel or skin they carry is inefficient at harnessing light. This disenchantment brought forth hatred but still a thirst for knowledge that declared that if there was no natural way to attain "enlightenment," then they would do everything in their power to attain it through artificial means.

What they did after they came into the information is exactly what they did when they came into contact with the people responsible for guarding that information. They would force upon the cosmic "symbols" a new language as well as upon the people responsible for guarding it, so as to place it in a state of flux. They would now see all their "symbols" in Latin and Greek and not in their native tongue, which they knew would have awakened the sleeping giant among those willing to seek out the true origins of themselves, their people, and the natural environment around them.

So, we should commit to memory that Karbon is Latin for *coal*. The six members of the Karbon family are Karbon, silicon, germanium, tin, lead, and flerovium. Remember they wanted to shroud this knowledge in mystery, so when you look at the Periodic Table of Elements you may ask, "If the element is named tin, why are the letters that represent the element Sn?" The reason why the letters that serve as the symbols are different from the name of the elements is because those letters represent the Latin name for the symbols!

Really think about this for a second. Latin is considered a dead language, not dead in the sense that no one speaks it; it's considered a dead language by linguists because a lot of people do not speak it, nor is it a language used in trade and everyday human activity. So how the language is classified now is by characterizing it as a liturgical language, which means this language is used for rites, rituals, religious ceremonies, etc.

So, one must ask themselves, "Why is a language that is used for rites and rituals being used to teach me anatomy and physiology, biology, and Khemistry?!" The reason is because they needed a way to give you just enough of the secret to keep you functioning but never enough to where you can create environments that nurture you to the highest level of autonomy. It's worth mentioning that no other family in the Periodic Table of Elements can make as many bonds as the Karbon14 group. All of the members of this family can make up to four bonds, as stated the most among any group in the "Table."

We know that *all* the names have Latin and Greek roots as well as *all* the letter symbols. The symbols that represent the elements are the Latin name for the element in question. Germanium is Latin for Germany; Karbon is Latin for coal; Silicon is Latin for hard rock; etc. So, as you see, when you possess the power to name something, it does not mean you know what it is but it does give you the power to determine what it means to others.

As I have said, think deeply for a moment, why is a "science," that even they say came from Khemit (hence the term chemistry), now spoken in a dead language? What also should be of importance, which many people overlook and don't understand if they have not taken such classes, is that the tough part is not learning the human body, the tough part comes into play when you have to learn another language in the process of learning the human body.

What more can you say about this creative force that can make stable bonds with other elements in an infinite set of arrangements bringing forth limitless outcomes and realities? In its elemental form, when it bonds only with itself, Karbon becomes what you know as diamond, which is the hardest natural substance known to humans, and it can become the softest material on earth when it is in the form of graphite. What is even more amazing is that as this cosmic energy transforms from one creation to the next, it exhibits totally different Khemical properties.

When Karbon is diamond, it is used as an insulator; when it is in the form of graphite, it can be used to conduct electricity. Diamond has the highest melting point at 3,550 degrees C. Imagine being able to turn your body into a substance that can resist extreme temperatures and conditions. This is the energy that the Most High has equipped you with! This is the reason for the disdain and disapproval that is shown by beings with compromised energy vessels, incapable of experiencing life at its acme of experience. This is the reason they placate you with sports, entertainment, and lifestyles that redirect your energy in fruitless endeavors only to find your windows of opportunities close on you because you have now gotten too old to be relevant.

Remember that eighteen of the thirty-four atoms that make up the melanin molecule are Karbon! The Blancos have said that they know of over ten million combinations so far that Karbon can make! Once again, I am going to announce through the bellows of Nature's horns that IF YOU DO NOT KNOW WHAT YOU ARE, YOU CANNOT POSSIBLY KNOW WHO YOU ARE! They have taken your birthright from you! You have languished for too long in mindsets that thirst for knowledge, among "leading" spirits that direct you to desert-like conditions.

They tell you that when Karbon interacts with nitrogen in the atmosphere it creates Karbon14, which is an isotope (an isotope is the *same* Khemical element with the same number of protons but a different number of neutrons). If situations arise where they should need to date an organism, they would use this form of Karbon in order to do it. This is important because I have stated countless times that we are *radioactive beings*!

If "organic khemistry" is the study of Karbon and we are Karbon beings that are not radioactive, then why would they use *radioactivity* to date Karbon organisms? So how the Blancos usually state said energy is in a way where the subliminal message makes the reader assume Karbon's "radioactive" form is Karbon14 and the other forms or isotopes of *naturally* occurring Karbon is not. We have to use this worldview carefully because *all* things in existence come about through the power of the electromagnetic spectrum and the spectrum is considered to be different manifestations of the same phenomenon, and the central source of *radiation*. Meaning radio waves, microwaves, infrared, etc., are all different aspects of the same phenomenon they call the electromagnetic spectrum.

All things emit radiation! We must refamiliarize ourselves with the energy that brought us into being and refuse to be taught about the mystery of ourselves through the lens of a people whose science and industries have reduced this planet to a shell of its former self. The Most High has demanded that you partake from the "Table" so that you may shed ignorance and feelings of inadequacy and in turn embrace what is resolute and literally invincible when the mind gives way to what is *natural*.

If you were keeping track of the "Table," you would also find the arrogance peppered throughout the Most High's manifesto. Out of the 118 elements of the Periodic Table of Elements, only 94 are naturally occurring elements, the other 24 are "radioactive" because they are unstable, created by humans. It is this instability that is really the term that accurately describes what the Blanco scientist fears, the fear of power acting irresponsibly with energy rooted in destructive behavior.

What they choose to tamper with in their labs was made by the Most High with balance and purpose in mind; what was made by humans is despotic and destructive in intent. As you look at the "Table," what you should know is that they are called groups or families because they exhibit the same behavior or have some of the same Khemical properties.

For instance, there was a time on my platform where I had mentioned a doctor who had healed herself by referring back to the "Table" and searching for answers there rather than from traditional outlooks. What she found was that her thyroid was not functioning properly because of excessive fluoride uptake. When she peered into the "Table," she realized the order among what seemed cryptic and detached.

When we isolate the halogen group, or Group 17, from the Periodic Table of Elements, we find that it is home to fluorine, chlorine, bromine, iodine, and astatine. As mentioned before, they have similar Khemical properties, so she realized that when the body does not have enough iodine available, then it will take up fluoride instead.

What must *always* be committed to memory is that as you go from *bottom up, left to right,* on the "Table" you increase in what's called electronegativity. When I listed the halogen group, they were listed from top to bottom, so you can easily surmise that fluorine is more unstable than iodine and because it is more electronegative and unstable, it will only lead to dysfunction within the thyroid, creating a hormonal imbalance that ultimately disrupts the endocrine system.

In all her years of studying health and the human body, it finally dawned on her just how important it is to go back to the basics and free yourself from third, fourth, and fifth levels of thinking; you begin to wrestle more with theories than dealing with absolutes. The doctor I mentioned is in the 2012 documentary, *The Great Culling: Our Water,* a film that is centered around the controversy of fluoride in drinking water.

Now that we know that these elements within these groups are "related," some very important observations should be highlighted and brought to our attention. Right below Karbon is silicon, the so-called second most abundant element within the earth's crust. When silicon bonds with oxygen, it makes silicon dioxide. This is quartz or sand. Remember the nickname for the Karbon14 group? We are called the "crystallogens." When these elements bond with one another they bond in crystal formation! As do all things that bond with Karbon because Karbon only bonds in a form called diamond cubic. Sand is what makes up glass; sand is also responsible for microchips. This is why they call their technological hub Silicon Valley.

The element that is under Karbon and *less* electronegative or less powerful is responsible for artificial intelligence (AI) technology. Does it not bother you that we are so removed from our true religion, the science of alkhemy, so much so that when we look at sand we think of death, scarcity, or at best the many walks on the beach during summer holidays? Our spiritual competitors who came out of Khemit with the true knowledge had awakened to something completely different. They realized the energy that can be harnessed when these elements begin to bond and transform into new building materials.

Where we just see sand now, they see glass and

microchips! Where we just see Karbon, they see products from margarine to plastics, creating industries that we have to work in, all because we are ignorant of the divine energy that brings life and meaning to this universe. When we breathe in oxygen, we chemically break apart the carbohydrate, splitting the Karbon and the hydrogen, creating water and Karbon dioxide to breathe out.

The idea that the Most High was and is in all things comes from this energy used to create and manifest all manner of phenomena in countless arrangements, yet the rightful benefactors have yet to undergo a paradigm shift, which would allow them to see just how far we are behind in our understanding and appreciation of such sacred power. Remember what they had taught you in their "schools," that fossil fuels, like coal and gas, come from decomposed plants and animals. They told you that the Koal or the Karbon came from decomposed plants from millions of years ago. They told you that the gas came from crude oil, which is found in the cracks of sedimentary rocks, their source being decomposed Karbon organisms.

What is it going to take for you to realize the amount of power that lays dormant inside of you? How are you not in awe that a gallon of Karbon can push vehicles that weigh tons down a road at maximum speeds? Why do you think they spend more time in the lab making your food than they do out in Nature? The reason is because they know full well the potential of Karbon and by hiding the true source of their leaps and bounds regarding Western evolution, all their accomplishments to the laypeople would appear to be feats only taken up by the gods.

This is why this occult "science" is expressed in a language that very few people speak fluently, a language used in religious rites and ceremonies because, as was stated before, our religion was our science! If you notice, it was the Blancos who figured that in order to cause confusion among the masses and an unavoidable existential crisis inside the individual, they would separate religion from science and they would become two different streams that claim to head to a larger body of enlightenment.

Let's see what happens when we use both "science" and "religion" to analyze the enigmatic forces around us. We've mentioned trees, so let us expound. When we take a look at the Garden of Eden, we say to ourselves, "Why would the Most High place us in a garden?" Logic tells us that there would be no better place on the planet to place the first two human beings than in a garden where they are around food so as to sustain themselves.

And when we use "science," it helps us to garner even more clarity on the issue at hand because we know that trees provide us with oxygen, and we breathe out Karbon dioxide. The trees not only provide food, but they also provide shelter and a calming place of refuge when the heat becomes unbearable. Its herbs consist of healing and restorative properties, keeping one's energy aligned with that of Mother Earth.

We should know by now that the world is ruled by signs and symbols and the story of the Garden of Eden is overshadowed by the fall from grace as human beings rather than the intimate and symbiotic relationship that exists between trees and the chosen people. Look it up for yourselves, the oldest trees in the world are off limits to laypeople, besides government officials, no one even knows the location of these magnificent trees.

Let's not forget when "Adam" and "Eve" were banished from the Garden of Eden, there were angels sent to guard the Tree of Life, preventing the couple from harnessing its power, for if they were able to go through with such an action, their minds would be open, allowing them to live forever.

"The man has now become like one of us, knowing good and evil. He must not be allowed to reach out his hand and take also from the tree of life and eat, and live forever" (Genesis 3:22, NIV).

Recall, it was only *after* they ate from the tree of knowledge that they knew the difference between good and evil, not before. So, why were they banished and given an order in the first place if they never knew the difference between good and evil to begin with? Of course, this is when most people who are stern believers begin to assert that "good and evil" now means something else entirely, and this sort of back-pedaling and side-talking is one of the reasons why most people are turned off by traditional religious systems and shallow-water swimmers who have no problem abusing authority from the pulpit.

What most of us did not take from that story is the relationship not only between the Most High and her human creations but also the relationship between plants and humans as well as between the plants and the gods! Remember, it was the Tree of Life that was said to grant everlasting life and not the Most High! The Most High plainly and directly states that she had already became "like them" in knowing "good and bad," when eating the fruit from one tree so there was no way she would allow them to live forever as the gods do themselves, by allowing them access to the Tree of Life.

As I have stated, trees that are sacred do not even have their location disclosed. We look at the Ring of Fire and witness the beauty and magnificence of giant redwoods that can live up to 2,000 years! Sequoias, giant trees that prefer the mountainous regions, can live up to 3,000 years! So, let's put this into perspective. The Most High places you in a "garden" where she tells you to be fruitful and multiply, instructing you on what trees you can take from and which ones you cannot.

You then partake of fruit from a tree that was forbidden and so your punishment was to be "banished" from the garden! Even before all of that, you were created with Karbon, which is Latin for Koal, and from what "science" says, it takes millions of years for this Koal to form (also stay mindful that this dynamic and divine energy is said to be decomposed plants), yet somehow something that was millions of years old in the making has found its way inside your skin and literally everywhere inside the body. If there is any place on this earth that is holding secrets, it is all placed within the confines of Nature.

We must revisit the powerful symbolism riddled throughout creation stories stolen from our ancestors. If the Bible was the manuscript that told of the beginning of human creation, the Periodic Table of Elements is the manuscript that gives the specific details of earth and humans in their perennial stages of development, while the Bible speaks in allegory at best.

Remember the tedious design behind the organization of the elements that they characterize as the building blocks of life. The horizontal rows reflect "periods," which in my strong opinion are symbols that also reflect "periods" of time! Let's not forget that they use radioactivity to date organisms (Karbon14), so the idea that these periods literally reflect a "moment" in time is not a baseless or farfetched claim.

It's also important to note that there are seven periods, reflective of the creation story most people are familiar with, the difference being "periods" and not "days!" According to the "Table," in the beginning, there was hydrogen and when you break down the element hydrogen, you come closer to understanding the true meaning behind this symbol. By employing the same stratagem to all the elements, you begin to weave together a story that is worthy of being called the greatest story ever written.

Hydro means *water* and the suffix gen means *generation*, as in first generation as well as the generating of energy. We all know that water is used to generate energy, hydroelectric dams, and nuclear power plants, but we rarely think of water producing fire because our thinking has always been that water puts out fire; it should never be able to produce it, one would think.

Remember the counsel that was given, we know that just because you can name something does not mean you know what it is! "Scientists" have no clue as to how "water" even exists in the form that you usually see it in, because there are many more compounds that have a greater molecular weight than water and they are still gases! So, in other words, they don't know why water, as light as it is, is not a gas instead of a liquid.

As we move forward, we see that the other element worth highlighting is all by itself as well. As I have said, the way the "Table" is designed is a way to bring it out for all those who have eyes to see. This element is helium. Its name is rooted in Helios, which is a name for the Sun. So, without haste but yet at the pace of royalty, the truth of the origins of the universe begins to make itself known to you.

The first "period" states that in the beginning the generating of water birthed a Sun! I know the skeptics will assume I am reaching beyond the length of the arms given me, but I assure you that I am well within reach, so much so that this truth is closer to my chest than my fingertips. There was a guy by the name of John Kanzius.

He came down with cancer and while recovering from chemotherapy, he envisioned a treatment. What he had found, seemingly by accident, was an origin story and not just an attempt to restore physical well-being by manipulating frequencies. Although he was only slightly off in his initial intent, he still came upon an incredible discovery.

He discovered that when you aimed a frequency at water, a frequency of 13.56 MHz, the hydrogen will split from the oxygen, and when a spark is lit, fire will come out of water! The fire will remain "birthed" out of the water as long as you aim that frequency at the water being manipulated. This phenomenon is called "the Kanzius effect." Not to mention, there are German myths that detail people running into an ancient weapon that they yield called the "flammenschwert," or "flaming sword," that would "react with the water," essentially a weapon that operates on a different frequency, which will ultimately affect water.

Once again, your perspective leaves you ill-equipped to notice what are obvious truths dangling in front of you. You are already aware that water is in the air, they refer to it as humidity. You already know that the molecular formula for water is H_2O. You also know that oxygen is extremely electronegative as they teach you in "Khemistry class" and that in order for fire to "breathe," it *needs* oxygen or the very element that is in the *water* in the air you breathe in!

Water is what keeps fire *alive*! From water birthed a Sun! What is also worth noting when you look at this alternate universe describing creation is the irony that radiates alongside the truth trapped inside the enigma. Helium, an element that they proclaim is a symbol in word that describes its connection to the Sun, is ironically used in cryogenics where you have to use very low temperatures, as well as how indispensable it is with X-ray machines, as the X-rays would degrade in the air if it was not for helium, as well as cooling machines used in this very same industry.

So, what should be of importance here is the irony regarding an element that in name reflects the Sun but in terms of Khemical behavior and its uses, we arrive at a conclusion that forces on us an entirely new meaning. This cycle will repeat itself the deeper down the rabbit hole you go, for all the obvious reasons. The first and most important is to ensure that you never get too close to seeing the matrix for what it really is, achieving true liberation, and the other is that they have to make themselves appear highly intelligent, justifying why they should be in the leadership role guiding humanity.

Those who are adept know this is an ingenious stratagem, one, because it allows you to admit that you don't know the answers and life is a mystery and extremely baffling, and two, that even without the answers the "scientific community" at least has the best guesses, which they agree on and then call them "theories" forcing the rest of humanity to acknowledge it until it transforms itself into conviction as we debate and disagree with one another. So even when we "eat from the Table" we can interpret the information in many ways and Blanco "science" does this to hide the truth from those who have access to the divine energy by birthright.

I will ask you again from the deepest wells of inquiry, how can these Blancos tell you how the universe started and yet they do not know when and where they came from? They are eager to tell you how the universe started millions of years ago, yet they are at a loss for words when it comes to explaining the origins of human life on earth. Notice, to fool you and keep the science, or better yet your religion hidden, they feign ignorance and proclaim humans may never know how it all began, creating scientific jargon to further confuse the layperson, making the journey of enlightenment more convoluted as you begin to realize the more questions you ask, the bigger their words become.

Oh, how we are so proud when our "intelligence" is validated by Blancos by receiving degrees, yet they can be self-taught or have no experience whatsoever in the field they choose to entertain at the moment and still operate within the court of public opinion with impunity. I have given you a couple of examples already, but I shall give another. Helena Blavatsky was self-taught and became respected in the world of existential thought. She started the Theosophical Society, where the cornerstones of this expression were built on Hermeticism (Hermes the Greek god and Thoth from Egyptian origin, respectively) and

Neoplatonic (think Plato) thought, which has a lot to do with alkhemy, which we know came out of Khemit and is the basis for the term Khemistry.

This brings me to my point, how someone who has no experience in the "science" of Khemistry, can then be given the authority to expound on second, third, and even fourth levels of understanding of said discipline without any blowback or repudiation from those who have been accredited with degrees given by hallow institutions. This is a huge part of the greater scheme of things, which allows Blancos to maintain control in every area of life activity.

The moment we relieve ourselves of the responsibility to learn of the world around us is the moment we abandon our rightful position in our cosmic lineage. It is the compartmentalization of information that exacerbates the issue at hand. How many of you can say that when educated in their "schools" that you have been taught with any of his textbooks from cover to cover? His system is one in which you start off on chapter one and skip to chapter five and then chapter twenty and by the time you have graduated they have told you that you are well-versed in what you know, even though you know they have not told you the whole story.

If I were to tell you a story and leave out names, dates, and details, how will you formulate an honest opinion about the matters at hand if you do not have all the necessary information available to you? This is the conundrum faced by all those endowed with the divine molecule melanin as they desperately search for knowledge to remain alive, because we all know that our people die due to lack of knowledge. Do you think it is by chance that these Blancos frame this information in a way that makes you feel disconnected from the science? Do you think it is by chance that they break the information up in "related" disciplines so that it becomes practically impossible to connect the dots?

As I have stated before, the way we look at the information from these "disciplines" is what will determine how far off we are at reaching the apex of awakening desired by students of the Most High. For instance, look at how you perceive the destructive energy that comes from weapons created by manipulating the Periodic Table of Elements. If you think of a hydrogen bomb, you usually think of the bomb itself and its destructive power, and not the atmosphere required to make the bomb the immense force that it was designed to be. Remember its radioactivity will be optimized by the oxygen and other particles in the air, just as a raging fire builds momentum due to the oxygen in the air.

There is energy all around us, an endless reservoir of potential that is overlooked because we have it stuck in our heads that these Blancos have not only monopolized the energy industry physically with interwoven infrastructures but also how we *perceive* this energy in terms of how it relates to us and its use. In other words, if you don't pay your energy bill, most people would be at a loss for how to generate power. Of course, you can use gas generators, which is another industry they control, or you can employ solar power and wind power, better alternatives but the startup can be expensive, to meet your needs, but we are here to go just a little deeper than that.

There is literally enough electrical energy in the air of your bedroom to power a whole neighborhood! Nikola Tesla had talked extensively of the importance of making sure that everyone in the world should realize that this power was ubiquitous and accessible to all, but the powers that be understood how much power was behind controlling the distribution of power. Even more important, as stated, was to control your perception of this power because it would place the people in a perpetual state of servitude when they believe power is scarce and can only be provided by big multinational corporations, which are "too big to fail." They have you believe when these giants collapse, where will you get the fluoridated water to drink, or the lab-created food to eat, or the toxic programs to watch?

Oh, how life will be dismal and return back to the Stone Age if we do not allow this hideous system to operate with omnipotence. Have you ever wondered why nearly all of their new discoveries may make it in their scientific journals and magazines but *never* make its way back into their textbooks? The reason for this is that you may find out the truth if you have exceptional analytical skills to speak of and an unrelenting spirit that has set out on a path to know the truth in its purest form, not through a myopic lens that says that one is just trying to find their place in society. That is what leaves you weak and vulnerable.

One must remember if you take this route, when things happen which are "outside of your control," you feel how truly powerless you are in the face of Nature, whether it be a natural disaster, or the human body breaking down. Regardless of the eventuality, the common denominator is the same, there is this darkened veil between you and Nature, which in turn aids in creating weak human minds, preventing the rise of energy that will enable an individual to achieve the status of demigod.

Have you not surmised by now that our lack of knowledge, or that specific body of insight that we die from when it is distant from us, has a lot more in common with Nature than with the little tricks and shortcuts people consume themselves with, what they say helps them navigate the turbulent waters of the Blancos anti-melanin matrix? Do they not control *Nature's* resources—wind, water, solar, and oil? Do they not control the very land you walk on by establishing boundaries and raising flags from the ground? Do they not tell you what you can legally consume, if they approve of it, and what punishment you will receive if you are in possession of something they do not?

A huge part of the veil's composition between us and Nature or the Metu Neter is the Blancos' legal framework and the language they decide to use to keep it spellbound to the melanated realm. If we feel like the energy all around us will only make itself known to us when the Blancos employ machines to serve as their mediums of expression, then we unwittingly and literally cut ourselves off from the Divine, relegating any notion of the Divine as thoughts that should only be entertained in science fiction novels or sci-fi movies.

This can no longer be the case if we are to flirt with the possibility of realizing our full potential. We must sit at the "Table" to understand why they have never allowed us to dine among ourselves. More important, it helps one to realize that the primary weapon wielded against us was not even religion, it is their "science!"

Earlier we discussed understanding the importance of elements being in groups or families and how a doctor found relief from her condition when she employed the wisdom from the "Table" to garner clarity. She found that iodine and fluorine are in the same family and that by limiting fluorine consumption and consuming a diet with foods rich in iodine, she was able to nurse her thyroid back to balance. This not only goes for health, but it also goes for war as well.

Let's take a look at the Karbon group again. What you notice is that lead is part of this group and is a metal. Because it is at the bottom of the group, it has a lower vibration and is toxic for beings of the Karbon family. There are numerous studies that were done showcasing how "people of color" absorb lead five to six times more than Hispanics and those of European descent. It's amazing to know that if I and a person with a lighter hue were in the same room, around the same source of lead, that lead would literally be more attracted to me than my counterpart.

They are fully aware that lead is at a lower vibration in our group and is extremely toxic to us and yet they make their ammunition out of this element. Isoprene is the compound that they use to make synthetic rubber, and rubber just so happens to be a compound that can trigger vitiligo. Vitiligo is a disease that attacks melanin.

So, this isoprene that can trigger melanin loss and cause sexual dysfunction, the Blancos conveniently enough put it in cigarettes, shoes, and the condoms you wear to "protect" yourself. I am not advocating unprotected sex, I am just proving that when you ignore Nature and let someone else tell you how the world works, you are at the mercy of their system, unfortunately.

There was a study done on isoprene, published in July 1994 by the National Institutes of Health (NIH) and the lead study scientist was Ronald L. Melnick, PhD. It reads as follows.

"In mice, exposure to isoprene caused decreases in hematocrit values, hemoglobin concentrations, and erythrocyte counts, atrophy of the testis and thymus, cytoplasmic vacuolization of the liver, olfactory epithelial degeneration in the nasal cavity, and epithelial hyperplasia in the forestomach" (Melnick, 1994).

So, it can cause shrinkage and poor function of the sexual organs; it can also cause an overgrowth as indicated by the term hyperplasia, with the difference being that these mice were inhaling the isoprene and we just so happen to wear it around our sexual organs. If you look at the date you should realize why those who are adept and can see are even more indignant because it is proof that they *already know* what they are doing and are keenly aware of the negative impact that these products will have on the targeted population as well as using our science, excuse me, our religion against us in order to manifest destiny.

See how when you eat from what is served at the "Table" that you begin to unearth what could not wait to be resurrected—the truth. Saint Augustine of Hippo said, "The truth is like a lion; you don't have to defend it. Let it loose; it will defend itself." By the end of this chapter you should have a greater understanding of Karbon, its role in the creation of the cosmos, its "king-like" nature, its ability to be indestructible when in diamond form or soft when transformed as graphite. It *only* bonds in crystal formation—called diamond cubic!

You should also commit to memory that the nickname for this family is the "crystallogens," as well as the chemical formula for melanin, $C_{18}H_{10}N_2O_4$, and how this formula is made up of the most "electronegative" elements in the "Table!" The way our melanin is structured within the vessels' landscape allows it to harness more of the energy from the central power source of radiation we call the Sun. Our essence is made of "diamond" or what is invincible, impenetrable against artificial means of intrusion. This is why the Blanco spends all his time in a lab reverse-engineering your wildlife in order to come closer to retrieving a weapon that can pierce the armor given by the Most High God.

How on earth can you listen to men who smile when they lie, who sleep like babies when they kill babies, and sadistically drew up a plan to have us complicit in the murder of Mother Earth by destroying her "Gardens" that we find ourselves banished from? If you had to abandon conventional life and survive within the confines of Nature, how lost do you imagine that most of our people would be? The chasm is so great that the Blancos can arrogantly proclaim that it would be an apocalyptic set of events that would transpire, all because they know they have been successful at capturing the mind of the melanated being, turning their "science" into a religion and their modern conveniences into neo-necessities.

It's amazing how most people never seem to understand the obvious about the Western thought process. Because of the information being compartmentalized, you begin to fill in the blanks with assumptions and not facts. What appears to be a seamless connection of linear thoughts and ideas is nothing more than cherry-picked events littered with bias taken out of a collage of cultural theft and barbaric social practices.

The point I am trying to make is this. If you were to ask someone if they believe in God or the Big Bang theory, a lot of people you know may submit to the creation theory and say that it was Almighty God who created the universe. Though when you ask them if they believe that the solar system exists (and I am not here to debate whether it does or not, that is, flat earth vs. round, just here to make a point), they will say they believe that planets do indeed exist because "scientists" have told us that they do. The problem with this approach is that one finds themselves in a position of serving two masters because according to biblical cosmology the earth is a dome!

"Let there be a firmament in the midst of the waters, and let it divide the waters from the waters" (Genesis 1:14 KJV).

You should remember that there is literally a "river in the sky," the jet streams and water in the atmosphere contribute heavily to atmospheric conditions. The Bible verse may be different in other versions, but all of them imply there is a firmament that separates the waters above from the waters below.

One should also note that the planets came about because of the Big Bang according to "science," so to be technical there is no belief in planets if there is no belief in the Big Bang. It's literally the cause according to "science" as to how the planets came about. Most in their haste will always try to reconcile the two (by saying God created the "heavens" or planets, or our ancestral evidence points to us using the stars) because as stated before our thought process is one in which we are taught chapters after skipping chapters, and, more important, religious institutions also have a tendency to transform their spiritual outlooks to remain relevant and influential to maintain power.

As stated before, this still does not take away from the idea that during the height of religious fervor, the known world subscribed to a geocentric model instead of the heliocentric model that most of us subscribe to today. Which means we always have to remember how important context is to understanding the path we see behind us. Without this analytical trait, we stand to sabotage the path we see in front of us.

So, remember it is incumbent upon Blanco "science" to prove they are telling the truth and not for me to prove them wrong. They are liars and liars deserve no advantages. Again, most people will focus on the debate between the "dome" vs. the "solar system" when the real question is why do we believe *anything* that comes out of these liars' mouths in the first place! How can you believe a man who has said 98.7 percent of human "DNA" is junk! They claim only the remaining 1.3 percent is the only part of our genome that is used for coding. Their "science" literally called it junk, because their science thought that it had or served no purpose.

The question you should ask yourself is, "Why would the Most High create us with a vessel that is almost 99 percent junk?" As always because mostly all of their worldviews are based on theory, you always hear or read statements that say things like "scientists once believed" or "scientists have now found that" or "scientists thought this species went extinct but . . ."

So as expected they double back and now tell us that the "junk DNA" is responsible for more activity within the body than previously held beliefs would suggest. Now all of a sudden this "junk" has stuff to do. They see that it is responsible for helping to fold the genetic material inside of the nucleus, but one could only assume that it's been decades since the discovery of "DNA," 1953 to be exact. How is it that it took so long for you to understand that the Most High does not create "junk"?! Also, why would you not change the name once you have been proven wrong.

What's even more perplexing is that their "scientists" have never seen "DNA!" The photo that was given to "scientists" James Watson and Francis Crick, men credited with the discovery, was a photo accurately titled the "UFO Photo." The photo was given to them from another "scientist," Rosalind Franklin. Yet the most incredible part about this story is that the process that was used to take the photo was a process called "X-ray crystallography," which is literally the *study of how crystals form*!

So now the question is, if they were not looking for crystals, why would they be using a method that studies how crystals form?! It should also be noted that the United Nations declared the year 2014 as the International Year of Crystallography. The way they see through the body is with X-rays. You must know X-rays are a part of the electromagnetic spectrum. The electromagnetic spectrum is a power source emitted from our central power source called the Sun, and radio waves, microwaves, infrared, visible light, ultraviolet light, gamma, and X-rays are all different aspects of these same phenomenon.

A combination of electricity and magnetism, this energy system is an interaction of waves and particles, starting off as waves primarily at the bottom with radio waves and then becoming more like energy as you heighten the vibration and reach X-rays. So, the point is, X-rays are too strong to get a snapshot of "DNA," so they have to settle with the images they claim are bounced back from the interaction with X-ray energy, and from this chemical interaction they surmise that "DNA" must be in the form of a double helix.

As stated before, when a people are known for being deceitful, there is no way that a reasonable mind should resort to interacting with such dishonest beings on an even playing field. If their "science" was crafted to heal and to "do no harm," why are there hundreds of thousands of deaths from people who take prescription medication the right way as instructed by their "doctor"? Why do innocent people have to galvanize their efforts and bring about class action lawsuits in order to receive judgments that fill their coffers with worthless paper money and no admission of guilt?

Fraud and medical malpractice are rampant in a world where both the doctor and the patient know very little about the medication that is being championed by Big Pharma. There is a lifelong obsession with experimenting with the "underclass" in order to curb population numbers and extract the godlike molecule from the Karbon baby, so that the elite can add days onto a frail, vile, and corrupted vessel.

The question still remains, how can we believe anything that comes out of the mouth of the Blanco? The reason why they will *never* be able to see what we look like at the molecular level, and I mean "we" as in eumelanin beings, is because at the molecular level our Karbon is designed to *absorb* light and not to reflect it! These so-called high-powered electron microscopes will never come close to peering into what should be an enigma by its design. Knowing that at its molecular level, it has the potential to be everything, why would it have form of any kind? This is called the personification of energy.

With their limited outlook, which we have adopted, they assume that even energy at its highest level has to have some likeness to human form. The main reason for it was obvious, that if you endorse this logic, those who forced this belief system on you stand to become gods themselves because, as stated in the Bible, humans were made in God's image. Because this is a foundational concept of creation, the only job left for the Blancos was to make themselves the reflection of that image.

Now this is where "science" creates problems for Blanco religion. If the Most High created two luminaries, one to rule the day and one to rule the night, why would the Most High create a luminary for the day that would cause cancer for the Blanco, if Blancos were the chosen people? How can the Most High, who represents the quintessence of light, accept a people on a spiritual plane of light when they cannot absorb the light on the physical plane? If Karbon at the molecular level absorbs all light and light is the spirit of the Most High in physical form, should we now start to look at the Karbon we possess as our direct link with the central power source of the Creator?

This is why in the Bible and in near-death experiences people speak of a bright light. We have already reviewed that the primary colors, when it comes to physics, are red, blue, and green. When these primary colors come together, they make a white light. So, in other words, our central power source that we know as the Sun coalesces the divine energy and distributes said energy to where it can be taken up in just the right amounts.

We already know that when a human harnesses the energy by making machines and gadgets to use the energy, it can be toxic. Like when Blancos take part of the spectrum to use the cell phone, microwaves are isolated and can be extremely harmful because now, it's not only in a concentrated source, that is, cell phone, it's also much more of these type of waves in the atmosphere. This is also one of the less popular "theories" supported by strong evidence as to why the bees are disappearing. Anytime it's the least popular outlook, it should raise some eyebrows because there may be more truth than fiction, plus we are all aware when the "scientific community" uses the word "theory" in a negative way, it usually means they are hinting toward the idea of a conspiracy theory so as to destroy any attempts at alternative outlooks gaining momentum.

This is why we have stated without reservation that Blanco "science" is so toxic. The creating of an artificial environment breeds imbalance throughout the ecosystem. The reason for this imbalance is because they are manipulating the "spectrum," that is, the Most High's energy, to carry out the insidious plans of the hidden agenda. They are fully aware that they are manipulating the "spectrum" in order to manifest an artificial environment that is imperative for Blanco survival as well as for the illusion that persists, which influences us to believe that evolution of the human species depends on Blanco "science" and not on the knowledge of Nature.

As stated before, how have the Blancos been able to convince you that something artificial is greater than what is natural? All they do is congregate in their labs and reverse-engineer Nature's technology and then claim credit for what always was and what will always be. Recall what we determined earlier: the way the information is presented will dictate how said information is perceived. Take blood, for instance, the technical name for blood is erythrocytes. Unfortunately, the way the Blancos explain this electrical phenomenon is to oversimplify it as a fluid that seems to just be responsible for delivering oxygen and nutrients throughout the body as well as taking the waste out of the cells and to prepare that waste for elimination.

Remember what we had stated earlier as well: that specificity is the key to understanding the matrix, not conclusions drawn from generalizing information. If we look at hemoglobin, we fail to realize that it is a compound term. *Heme* is an organic ring, or a porphyrin ring that is designed to *"absorb light!"* *Globin* is considered the protein, but when you put the heme and the globin together, you get hemoglobin. Heme is an organic ring, made up of four pyrrole subunits; pyrrole is what is characterized as a "heterocyclic aromatic organic compound."

I hope you have also noted that the closer you get to the truth, the bigger the words become that are used by Blanco "scientists." There are no worries here, melanated gods and goddesses, because when you dig deep it not only serves as a way to enlighten the darkened mind, it also can serve as a grave for the opposition when all that needs to be known is unearthed.

"Heterocyclic" just means that there is more than one element inside the "ring," or "cycle" and these would be elements such as Karbon, hydrogen, and nitrogen, and the way in which they bond, they make a ring. You may be familiar with "aromatic," which suggests odor although not all "aromatic" rings have odor. In Khemistry, this just refers to "hydrocarbons" and the rings that can develop, because you must commit to memory that especially in regard to energy sources, hydrogen and Karbon are the most sought after and they refer to these bonds as hydrocarbons.

Last but definitely not least is the term "organic compound." This is a compound where Karbon is an indispensable part of the molecule. But what else is new, right? We already know that the study of *everything* on this so-called planet has to mention Karbon if the inquiry is to produce satisfactory results. Simply put, life is the study of "organic Khemistry" or "Karbon Khemistry" if you will.

When the oxygen or the "air" interacts with this "ring" it now brings "color" to what was previously a colorless volatile liquid. The Karbon absorbs the "light" or radiation and brings color to the blood. Imagine if there was no color to the blood? Think about how hard it is to get the color of blood out of fabric and how forensic investigators use a substance called luminol to see traces of blood at crime scenes, because the luminol reacts with the iron in the heme molecule so as to illuminate the blood.

So, the Karbon absorbs the light, and the iron in the blood acts as a conductor of electricity, because that's what metals are good for. This is why Khemistry is amazing! People talk about robots and how they are made of metals and wires and fail to realize that we are not that much different at all, we just happen to have the elements in different amounts and bonded with other elements, which brings about different shapes.

In Khemistry, it is a well-known rule that shape determines function. If there is not enough of this "metal" in your blood, you will have a hard time capturing "oxygen" and mental and physical fatigue will set in and you will become anemic. This metal also plays a huge role in turning the blood red; we see what oxygen does to iron outside of the body for reference. Over 70 percent of the iron in the body is in the blood.

The blood is made in the bone marrow and in order for you to have strong bones, you need vitamin D. Vitamin D is called the "sunshine vitamin" and you obviously get it from the Sun. So, the logic goes if you cannot be in the Sun, then you cannot make strong bones, which in turn you cannot make healthy blood. Just look up the history of the Blancos in relation to blood transfusions and you will understand all too well where I am going with this.

So, what the Blancos did, through their science, is marginalize the true role of blood, all the while getting you to donate the life force to the elite so as to keep these beings inside of the dome until they discover artificial means of keeping their vessel viable. Most people think this is conspiracy talk until you show them the proof from the "Table," and when you look at the "Table" all will be made known to you.

Fifty-five percent of blood is plasma, and if you notice when people go to donate "blood," the elite take the "plasma" and discard the rest of the blood. The reason for this is because it's not blood at all, if anything it is just plasma!

Think about this for a second, critically. If a man owned a business and he had a 55 percent share in the company, would he not be seen as the one with the most power in that relationship? So why is it these Blancos lose their attention to detail when it comes to the metaphysical? If 55 percent of blood is plasma, that represents the majority. How is the majority of its makeup ignored, and it is known by its lower form of makeup in terms of composition?

What you need to know that is critically important is *plasma is known as the fourth state of matter*! The three states of matter most people are familiar with are solid, liquid, and gas. So why do we not hear much of anything about the fourth state of matter, *plasma*? The big difference between plasma and gas, is that plasma is *electric*! Recall as we said Blanco "science" desires for you to have a shallow understanding of plasma so that it makes it easy to give away to these vampires, but the truth is, it is the energy that flows through you so as to allow the whole vessel to take part in the transformation process in the event that the highest level of enlightenment is attained.

Remember, they say plasma is what created the universe by virtue of a Big Bang and that after the plasma cooled, planets began to form. When you ask a Blanco "scientist" in one of his/her classrooms about plasma, all they tell you is that it is a light yellow liquid that has water, salts, enzymes, antibodies, and other proteins, not that it is affected by electrical and magnetic fields, another key part of its character that essentially separates it from a gas.

Recall how water is a big part of blood and/or plasma. Ninety-eight percent of blood is supposed to be water. Notice how I said, "supposed to be," because we must always remember we are only as much water as we drink, not what they say the body is. This is the slick way they sell a lot of "water-based" products, because you are under the assumption that you can drink something with water in it, even if it's just flavored water and you have taken care of your daily needs, but nothing could be further from the truth.

There is a concept called "free water," basically water that has a job to do. When you consume flavored waters and "water-based" beverages, these types of water products already have a job. Water can make bonds, actually water is capable of dissolving more substances than any other liquid known to humans, thus the title "universal solvent." So, when water makes chemical bonds with all these additives in the "flavored water,' only water can break these bonds, which puts the body in need for "free water" to accomplish that task.

The body has many ways of conserving water and compensating for the primary source of energy, and one way is by influencing the organism to use less energy. Coffees, teas, alcohols, and colas are well-known diuretics, which only means they release your free water crucial for maintaining normal energy levels within plasma.

So now do you see the real reason why the Blanco mad "scientist" contaminates the water? Look at what we have established already from looking at "blood" in a different "light," if you will. We found out that it is primarily plasma, and this plasma is the fourth state of matter and is primarily electric gas, and this electric gas is mostly made up of water. Logic would dictate that inside the body of the Karbon being is a type of water that interacts with a metal called iron, absorbing light and distributing this light all throughout the body, transporting not only nutrients and waste products, but thoughts as well, communicating inside and outside of cells.

Blancos call these systems your endocrine and nervous systems, respectively. So, because you have been taught in a way where the magnificent and wonderful have been reduced to the insignificant and mundane, then it stands to reason they will continue having no problem getting you to give the fourth state of matter away for some worthless paper money. It should amaze us even more that when we factor in that water, according to its molecular weight, is not even supposed to be a liquid but a gas, and that this "liquid" when subjected to a frequency of 13.56 MHz can split apart and produce fire, now you begin to tread among waters that come closer to identifying what you are, so you can fully understand *who you are.*

When you come to know the many properties of water and Karbon, the supernatural is not so farfetched, it actually becomes something you can feel, thus motivating every fiber of your being to commit, with the conviction and expectation of turning these divine thoughts to reality. The reason we should remain confident that these things can happen is because Nature has already shown us what other organisms can do when they have to do so for survival!

Recall that necessity is the mother of invention. The animals in Nature are using the *same energy* as we are using (because they are made up of the same stuff), just in different ways so as to ensure survival in their environments. We see it in the evidence of the matrix that was built off the back of Karbon and the millions upon millions of combinations made by Karbon with other elements within the "Table."

Once again, when you look at the "Table," everything becomes clear to you, especially in terms of elucidating *why* there is so much hatred toward the people who contain the godlike molecule that we know as melanin. When you look at the many other uses for these elements and the properties they have when you manipulate their "Khemistry," you now see the Blanco position as the energy diametrically opposed to the natural reign of Karbon would be beyond questioning.

Look at the Halogen group. They are *reactive* nonmetallic elements that form strong compounds with hydrogen that are acidic. These elements are fluorine, chlorine, bromine, iodine, and astatine. Now, were you aware that fluorine is in fluorescent lights? Halo is Greek for *salt* and gen obviously means to *generate*. So, in other words, salts are ionic compounds, or charged compounds that "carry" the electricity through water. This is why they can sur-round the filament inside of a light bulb with vapors of a halogen element and produce electricity, yet you just see iodine as being a "nutrient" for the thyroid. Meanwhile, the Blancos are in their labs finding new uses for the same "nutrient," thus the term "halogen lights," while you just associate it with keeping an organ healthy.

Just like you assumed that sand was only good for long walks on the beach and notorious for getting between your toes, the Blancos have turned it into glass and microchips that power their artificial matrix. Can you see now it's not as simple as reading a book if you cannot understand what you have read. I was told by a very wise melanated soul who used to be a schoolteacher in the Baltimore area, that "if you cannot understand what you have read, then you, sir, cannot read."

When you see life's mysteries through the lens of Khemistry, the veil is lifted. The degrees that the Blancos offer from their institutions are nothing more than added layers on the onion of truth. One knows full well if you take classes for a science-based degree, the classes seem to blend because so much of the information is related. The problem is the high level of skill at which the Blancos operate in terms of manipulation. The secret to their rec-ipe is giving *one thing, many names.*

An example of this is the banana. The banana is radio-active, so much so that at one point of time bananas were used as a measurement of radiation for Blanco "scientists."

A banana contains potassium, which according to the "Table" is a soft silvery-white *metal*. If we are to be specific, a banana contains potassium-40, this is the reason it "spoils," or in the world of Khemistry, this is the element causing the banana to start *radioactively decaying*!

So, the point is, when you take a class on "nutrition," the banana is spoiling, but in the world of Khemistry, the banana is radioactively decaying! The way the information is relayed to you will determine how you interpret it! Most of the elements, formulas, and natural phenomena I have discussed with you up to this point, you already are aware of, but it is the recognition of its other attributes that has lit the fire of curiosity.

Blancos have become so confident in their quest for domination that they can place the "Table" in a game and become one of the most popular games of its time. Always keep in mind the best place to hide information. For instance, when Karbon bonds *only* with itself, it forms diamonds. This is the purest form of Karbon, and this is why it is the most sought-after jewel by Blanco mineral thieves.

When you take a look at silicon, which is also in the Karbon14 group, you find out when it bonds to oxygen, it becomes silica dioxide and forms quartz! Then you have the rest of the "cardinal gems." Ruby is corundum or aluminum and oxygen bonded together; amethyst is a violet quartz; sapphire is another version of corundum, that is, aluminum and oxygen but with trace amounts of other elements like magnesium, iron, and vanadium, etc.

Because we have already mentioned diamond, which is the most sought after, the only one left is emerald, which is beryllium aluminum cyclosilicate, a fancy mashup of the Khemical elements beryllium, aluminum, and oxygen but the element chromium is what gives it its green color. Aquamarine is also a well-known variety of beryllium.

Diamond is the most treasured to the Blanco, because it is considered *pure*! When crystals are bonded with other elements that don't make up a significant amount of the crystal, then those elements are considered to be "impurities." So, diamond is treasured among those who plunder, because it only needs to bond with itself in order to achieve perfection, needing *no other elements in the "table!"* I hope from this you have committed to memory the importance of understanding that *everything* in this realm only bonds in crystal formation, because everything contains Karbon, and Karbon *only bonds in a crystal formation called "diamond cubic!"*

As I've stated before, the reason why they can hide this in a game and then you subconsciously become attracted to that game is because it resonated with you on the molecular level. Our Karbon vessels contain the secrets of the universe; they shall never be able to hide such things from us forever. I'm pretty sure you are impatiently waiting to discover what game I'm referring to that hides the secrets to life in plain sight. That game was Tetris!

Tetris is Greek for *four*, referencing the "cube," and the dead giveaway is when you bond different shapes along with colors you create "gems." It's rare that you receive the cube, which represents Karbon and the mini-cubes, which are fused together to make a straight line (representing the Karbon/hydrogen bonding), because that would make the game too easy and, more important, you wouldn't get the variety of gems that are created by mixing and matching the elements. The game Tetris is literally a crude representation of the "Table" and its power to form life-forms using crystals as building blocks.

As was stated earlier, because Blanco "science" only places emphasis on crystal formation when it comes to "gems," it never dawns on people that the rules cannot change just because we are "human." There are no exceptions! All things that contain Karbon are an end result of crystal formation, hence the reason for X-ray crystallography being used as the tool for investigating "DNA," not to mention the nickname for the Karbon family is the "crystallogens!"

The Blancos "science" has us waiting for great and overwhelming energy to be bestowed on us from above or in some cave deep in the Tibetan mountains, but the Most High has assured you that her divine energy is *everywhere*! I read an excellent book years ago as my awakening process began to take effect. Even though as of now I don't submit to some of the terms that are used, the message was loud and clear. In a book titled *The Biology of Belief,* written by Bruce H. Lipton, who has a PhD, by the way, just in case your Oreo senses are going haywire with me as a Black man explaining what is hidden to you. He stated,

"There are lots of IMPs [integral membrane proteins] with lots of different names, but they can be subdivided into two functional classes: *receptor proteins* and *effector proteins*. Receptor IMPs are the cell's sense organs, the equivalent of our eyes, ears, nose, taste buds, etc. Receptors function as molecular 'nano-antennas' tuned to respond to specific environmental signals" (Lipton, 2008, 53).

He goes on further to state that

"Receptor 'antennas' can also read vibrational energy fields such as light, sound, and radio frequencies. The antennas on these 'energy' receptors vibrate like tuning forks. If an energy vibration in the environment resonates with a receptor's antenna, it will alter the protein's charge, causing the receptor to change shape" (Lipton, 2008, 53).

As stated before, when you alter shape in Khemistry, you change function! The energy is *everywhere* and yet we have been forced to believe one or two things: it will come from a source hidden or not yet revealed that is outside of us, or the energy is inside of us and has yet to be tapped into. Why the division? Are not both of them true? See, the sooner we become one in knowing the behavior of energy in this realm, the closer we become to making our wildest imagination a reality.

In my current state, terms like physics and quantum physics are merely euphemisms for the religion (alkhemy) that was stolen from us and turned into a "science." So, as I have said, I do not agree with every term used by "scientists," but I understand the intent. Many times when the Most High leads you to certain sources, the point is to look at things in terms of what impact it has had on your psyche. The message for me that I remember at the time after reading this work was clear as day, and that was to question *everything*!

Why would you not question everything, when someone who had spent their whole life teaching Blanco "science" had suddenly had an epiphany and began to realize the source of their disconnect from Nature was none other than the tool used to teach them about Nature.

Lipton goes on to state,

"Physics, after all, is the foundation for all the sciences, yet we biologists almost universally rely in the outmoded, albeit tidier, Newtonian version of how the world works . . . there are no absolutes. At the atomic level, matter does not even exist with certainty; it only exists as a tendency to exist. All my certitudes about biology and physics were shattered" (Lipton, 2008, 89).

Do you see how when you stick to the alkhemical chart those second, third, and fourth levels of understanding become merely a play on words and the running of mental laps, which are nothing but exercises in futility. Are you aware that the Blancos characterized this era of human existence as the "sixth wave of extinction"?! Why should we be led by individuals who always appear to be on a suicide mission, suffering because of the overreliance on nonrenewable resources, monoculture farming techniques, which lead to more pathogens and disease, deforestation and the overfishing of oceans, not to mention the inherent hatred for the people who were chosen to protect this realm at all costs when the time comes.

Now is that time, beloved. You have been dealing with a being who has made a habit out of telling you half-truths and outright lies until you feel that the solutions, which may remedy your chaotic life, are a million miles away, when they have always been all around you. When the information brings forth new meaning, then life will naturally submit to a new meaning as well. How long will they keep the real you from surfacing? The answer lies in the level of aggression you use to acquire the truth.

When we go back to the blood, or "plasma," if you will, to be used as an example, you can see clearly just by the type of equipment used to remove any doubt of them knowing exactly what you are. If you have ever had more than a few hospital visits regarding breathing issues or you are a woman and have had a child birthed at a hospital, then you are familiar with a device called a "pulse oximeter." How it works is they shoot small beams of light that pass through the blood in the finger, measuring your oxygen levels, and the *changes of light* in blood that has been oxygenated and blood that has been deoxygenated is what helps them to acquire a more accurate diagnosis.

What did we proclaim earlier without this strong piece of evidence even being considered? We stated that the primary responsibility of "blood" or plasma is to absorb light, and by them monitoring the absorption rate of light by the blood with this device, it allows them to determine what the next course of action would be for someone who may not be utilizing oxygen efficiently.

Imagine being able to utilize different forms of light, like our ancestors of the distant past, to heal and to diagnose imbalances within the human body. Of course, this may seem unbelievable to those who wait on the Blancos to put it in a movie and then come out with a special six months later on National Geographic detailing how new discoveries in "science" have now moved into the realm of sci-fi. They do this so you will associate them with gods, so you never question what comes out of their labs and their think-tank operations.

Are you aware that they have added four new elements to the "Table," completing the seventh period! Elements 113, 115, 117, and 118 will get their names soon, and this has been declared by the International Union of Pure and Applied Chemistry. Have we not already discussed that new elements bring about new life or what many also refer to as "elemental beings"? The reason they said the seventh period was not complete was because the period had consisted of elements the "scientific" community had not properly studied yet.

Considering that these elements are humanmade, who gives these beings the authority to bring other life-forms to this realm without our approval? I guarantee they will soon speak about how life-forms they thought were extinct have now reemerged and have the "scientific" community in a tailspin. When they are in their labs, they are not in there to come out with anything that will benefit the people who they know have been given all they needed from the Most High. What we do know is they are in there reverse-engineering Nature to create a more hospitable existence for those who rule in darkness and with a heart ruled by envy.

They uses white mice in their labs because of the lack of pigment they have, even though the mouse has very little in common with the physiology of human beings. They are resistant to certain toxins, they don't have the complementary pathway in the blood, nor do they have as many white blood cells as we do, yet over 75 percent of the time this is the animal Blancos choose to experiment with to push out prescription medication and medical advice and guidelines.

Not too long ago, "scientists" had developed a drug that "mimics" sunlight and was said to give you a brown tan without being exposed to harmful UV radiation.

"The drug tricks the skin into producing the brown form of the pigment melanin in tests on skin samples and mice. Evidence suggests it will work even on redheads, who normally just burn in the sun. The team at Massachusetts General Hospital hope their discovery could prevent skin cancer and even slow the appearance of ageing" (Gallagher, 2017).

Once again, why would a people who claim that the Bible was about them, leaving the impression that they were *born perfect*, made in God's image, be born without the very thing that would allow them to live a perfect existence? If they thought that their skin was a part of the "blessing" that the Most High had bestowed on them, why are they in their labs experimenting with mice so they can acquire not just a tan, but, more important, a Khemical bond with the melanin so it can "protect them" from the "harmful" UV radiation and give them a more youthful looking appearance?

Notice the words they use when they describe our central power source, the Sun. They use terms that would suggest to laypeople that this luminary is a vile and dark form of energy that people need protection from. Recall, as I have mentioned, that if they were blessed with the supercharged form of Karbon, eumelanin to be specific, you would never hear the end of how intimately connected they are with the Divine. I guarantee you that there would be no other elements in the Periodic Table of Elements, just Karbon and its ability to transform into many other elements, not bond with many other elements, a difference which is chiefly responsible for why you marginalize and underestimate the power of Karbon.

We see it in the evidence given above, because as they have noted, if they can create a Khemical that allows them to absorb the Sun's rays without the burning and other adverse health effects, then this would change their experience and allow them to live without the envy and indignation that they have for those who have inherited the "image" of the Most High.

We speak of the Sun as if it does not produce Karbon. Are you aware that there is a Khemical process that this celestial body goes through inside itself, which produces the element that is responsible for all life on Mother Earth? According to Blanco "science," it is the explosion of stars that brought and continue to bring Karbon and oxygen into the universe, not the Big Bang. This nuclear fusion reaction, which also occurs in our Sun, is a dynamic display in energy transformation where three helium-4 nuclei are transformed into Karbon in an event called the triple-alpha process.

So, if the Sun's main job is to make Karbon, is it not safe to assume that it is a Karbon star? As I have stated before, and will many more times in the future, if this was the element that was key to their material and spiritual makeup, of course the central power source would be a Karbon star! The problem is because it is not an integral part of their essence, then you have to settle for digging deeper, using etymology as a tool to get closer to discovering the real meaning of life.

There was an article published by *BBC News* in 2004. The title of the article was "Diamond Star Thrills Astronomers." A "scientist," astronomer Travis Metcalfe, was quoted as saying,

> "We figured out that the carbon interior of this white dwarf has solidified to form the galaxy's largest diamond . . . Astronomers expect our Sun will become a white dwarf when it dies 5 billion years from now. Some two billion years after that, the Sun's ember core will crystallise as well, leaving a giant diamond in the centre of the solar system" (*BBC News*, 2004).

The "scientist" being interviewed caps it off by saying, "Our Sun will become a diamond that truly is forever" (*BBC News*, 2004). Do you honestly think for one odd second that these maleficent beings will wait five billion years for this to take place? If they are here consuming Karbon beings at a rate too fast to keep track of, how much longer before they turn their hatred toward *our Sun*?!

Do you think that it is just by chance that these Blancos commemorate their unions with the diamond when they marry each other? Of course, as of now we have taken on their practices, but these are rituals they engage in to harness power against the "crystallogens." Our people were and still are the greatest thinkers on earth! So, if we were the first scientists, doctors, astronomers, etc., then why is there no history of us undertaking campaigns around the globe, cutting down trees, digging up oil and coal, and destroying delicate ecosystems, proclaiming that this was the only way to build "advanced civilizations."

This is why the greatness of our people perplexes the Blancos, because they have to admit there was a Divine power that was used and tapped into, a power that was aligned with Nature, a power that was innate and given to the vessel at birth as a gift *apart* from the "conscious mind." This vessel allowed us the freedom from burdening ourselves with the pursuit of higher technology, because *we were and still are the technology*!

The vessel was already equipped with the knowledge of Nature! It keeps track of trillions of cells, yet the conscious mind says that it is not good at math. It creates light inside of your mind so that you can "see" your dreams, yet the conscious mind says that you can only see when the Sun is out. It never forgets to breathe for you, heal you when you are cut, and fight off infections when you are sick, because it has one job and one job only, to tell you all of the universe's secrets when you are ready. Is this not the other half of the proverb, which starts off as "Know thyself"?

This is why Blancos bombard your mind with sub-liminal messages through religion and secular thinking, that this vessel is made from dust, too flawed to get you to the acme of enlightenment. That the body was born in sin, inherently disconnected from the Creator until the day of judgment has passed and a long-awaited spiritual government establishes itself. I tell you this is fallacy! These are nothing but spells that were passed down to them to ensure the arrested development of the melanated warrior.

Can you see now how important it is to revisit foundational concepts so that you can juxtapose them next to what Nature has taught you about life? I guarantee from this vantage point you will see without a doubt how their "school" curriculum falls apart in the face of empirical evidence. You can no longer allow them to define what this Divine energy is. Their "scientists" have convinced us that "artificial" intelligence is greater than natural intelligence.

How is it that when you think of the afterlife you see yourself as having to leave the vessel to get to the light, when Nature has designed the vessel to absorb light?! Recall that the Blancos have to convince you that your gold is worth nothing, and this is how they are successful on a spiritual level in giving you their worthless paper for your gold.

Instead of training the mind to leave the body to get to the light, train the mind to get to the light through the body. Crafting a new narrative is critical to changing the function of the melanin molecule. Instead of you using it as a political statement, (that is, Black Lives Matter, Black Power, etc.), it should be used for what Nature gave it to you for, and that is the absorption of radiation coming from the central power source called the Sun, so as to behold great wonders and to be of great service to the Most High.

In Blanco society, they have reduced your vessel to the lower ranks of physical attraction, increasing or decreasing according to shade, yet say nothing about how magnificent it is in terms of light absorption! Through the eyes of Nature, for one to get closer to the highest level of life's experience, you must get darker, yet in Blanco society, in order to get closer to "easy street" you must become lighter.

We must redefine our energy so it can become our defense among Moon worshippers who are in a perpetual state of bloodlust. You now know the importance of Karbon, its Khemical makeup, it's group or family, in addition to its role in the universe as well as its potential to uncover the biggest secret hidden from the Karbon baby.

PART 2

The Greatest Lie Ever Told to Us

From the cryptic lives of sages to the lower levels of closed-door gossip, life proves time and time again that anything worth knowing in life always starts off as a secret. Now that you understand more about the godlike molecule melanin, you come one step closer to realizing its full potential, as well as elucidating the real reason why *all* nations on earth have conspired against you. Every "elite" nation in the Western bloc as well as those powers that stand at the fringe of inclusion, have agreed on a history that further distances the melanin beings from their true and only one identity, and that is a Krystal people, who *absorb light*, not by virtue of conviction via conjecture, but by evidence via Nature!

What was fiendishly desired by Blancos was the arrested development of this chosen class by indoctrinating them with the inexhaustible lows of bondage. All we hear from Blanco historians as well as Boule gatekeepers are the horrors of slavery, the indelible impact on the psyche of melanin beings due to its legacy and their commitment to making it the most significant part of our identity.

If I were to tell most Black folks that my people were not slaves, they were always free, albeit paying the highest price to assure that freedom, they usually show a look of disgust. If there is a verbal response when I say that my people were not slaves, most of the time I get a response like, "Nigga, you Black, ain't you?" It seems the only time we are not talking about slavery is because we are now probably talking about reparations.

See, unlike you, I am fully aware that those of my bloodline were warriors, fending off a new organism that won wars against us not because of their material weapons, but because of their biological ones. When the "conquistadors" set off on their voyages, they took their feral (wild) pigs and dogs with them. Feral pigs are still a problem today with millions in the South and the Southeast regions, spreading disease and compromising ecosystems, a highly invasive species because it has no known predators after two weeks of age. Then it was the Blanco dogs, which are a vector species known to carry rabies. The Blancos used the wild pig as food and the wild dog as a companion in warring against the indigenous.

Most are just familiar with the story of blankets infected with smallpox, but the truth is the Blancos were a vector species themselves: smallpox, typhus, syphilis, to name a few. Syphilis was initially called the "French disease," or the "Polish disease," or the "German disease," depending on which country blamed its neighbor for the outbreak. Then officially it was named syphilis in 1530 by an Italian physician named Girolamo Fracastoro. You have to get rid of the anachronistic outlook where you visualize the Blanco man with the guns he has now, and the land he has annexed into his empire today to reimagine the past. His main weapon was disease and much of the land that he found himself on was already occupied by Nature's people.

"From the 15th to the 18th century, smallpox epidemics were endemic to Europe. The Spanish introduced smallpox to the New World early in the 16th century, and within decades, the disease produced extreme mortality among the indigenous peoples. By 1600, 9 out of 10 South American natives succumbed to European diseases" (Faragher, 1998, 863).

Bartolomé De Las Casas wrote a book called *A Short Account of the Destruction of the Indies,* detailing the horror and documenting the abuses of the natives as they were literally dropping like flies. It was the Blanco ancestors who possessed wild animals and released infected convicts and bloodthirsty suicide packs to subdue regions where the number of people of color had to be significantly reduced, then subsequently forced into a mental prison by a foreign tongue. This in turn would sever our ties from Nature, leaving spirituality in a shell of its former self, losing more and more of itself as it buys into the idea of its origin as a religion.

I'm sure no one would be surprised in knowing that religion is a tool used to govern oneself, so by default a "government" would only be a spitting image of that authority. Did not the Quakers build the first institution in Philadelphia in 1773 calling it the Walnut Street Prison with the intentions of punishing criminals until they deemed them fit to re-enter society? All religion did was rent the house until "science" could take over the lease.

There are many "Christian colleges" that offer law degrees, which is a field that blatantly intersects with the political and social "sciences" more so than with religion, but when you heighten your analytical skills, you begin to realize that religion and "science" have been working together all along, shattering the perception of this narrative of a centuries-long hatred for one another as they would lead us to believe.

Science picks up where religion left off. The reason for this is because they knew they had to cover up their origins for fear that those being manipulated by them presently would become giants after an involuntary slumber. When you peer through the "Table," you begin to realize, on a Khemical level, if nothing can exist in this realm without the power of Karbon, these organisms are nothing more than a "genetic experiment" spun out of control.

Recall from their "science," they tell you that *all* organisms are made of the same "four nitrogenous bases" referred to as adenine, guanine, cytosine, and thymine as well as uracil if you are counting "RNA." It is the order or "sequence" they are in, which determines the organism, hence the term "sequencing DNA." These bases are organic compounds or compounds containing Karbon and are in the same class of compounds that make up the heme ring in blood, which is responsible for storing light, a term we have already discussed and defined, as "heterocyclic aromatic organic compounds."

They place adenine and guanine as a "purine," and they place cytosine, thymine, and uracil as "pyrimidines" (notice the association to the word pyramid in the last symbol). As we have proved and will continue to prove time and time again, Blancos are extremely efficient at destroying clarity because they use many names for one phenomenon. These "compounds" are nothing more than the many faces of Karbon as it chooses to arrange itself under the direction of cosmic laws so as to become different aspects of reality.

What needs to be of the utmost importance here is the understanding that it is the "mixing" of these "compounds" that bring about new organisms! If Blancos are still in awe of those responsible for building the pyramids and have abandoned the concept of linear progression relating to technically advanced civilizations, would it not stand to reason that our ancestors knew how to manipulate life on earth, in an effort to become like the Most High?

When we hear about them in their labs successfully creating human/monkey embryos, do we not have the same reaction the Most High would have? A reaction that without hesitation says that you are meddling in a power that is far beyond your level of understanding. This meddling is what leads to disruptions in Nature's course and the exact reason the vanguards of this realm have found our lives and our future on the edge of extinction.

We are ready to commit to the idea that the Blancos have been playing god as they continue to push the envelope regarding "genetic engineering," but we hardly ever accept that if we were the gatekeepers of this knowledge to begin with, we would have inevitably suffered from the same complex as well. Remember it is called Khemistry! The manipulation of the Khemical elements is how *all* technological advances are made, while the ignorance of them is the veil that separates gods from men.

So, if we held the knowledge that could lead to manipulating Nature, does it not make sense to have measures in place that would prevent the circumstances we currently find ourselves and the world in? We as a people continue to wonder if the stories of the past involving "genetic manipulation" were true. Yet right before our very eyes they show you or write down in "science" articles and magazines that are peer reviewed of their many advances in manipulating life. And because there is nothing new under our Sun and there is historical evidence like the pyramids to prove that advanced civilizations existed, we must remove ourselves from the notion that Blancos were and are the only reason humanity has "evolved" at the rate we have.

They have told you of the beginnings of the science by naming it after where it came from, then they used this science, which was your spiritual manuscript, to build the artificial matrix that you see in front of you. The reason they have been successful in stealing this information is because you do not realize the value of what it is that you are surrendering.

- Where most Black people see a couple of pints of worthless blood, the Blancos see the fourth state of matter called plasma that they can reverse-engineer in their labs and study.
- Where most Black people only see their newborn baby boy's foreskin, the Blancos see something called foreskin fibroblasts that sell for $150,000 and is placed in Blanco makeup to keep them looking younger.
- Where most Black people just see sand, the Blancos see glass and the microchip, which the latter of the two has been the cornerstone of their evolution stepping into the twenty-first century.

It's the equivalent of the experiment of giving a naïve child two quarters for the dollar you initially gave them, simply because they have yet to think in an abstract way, realizing that two isn't always greater than one. This devaluation of our inheritance was necessary to stay close to their food and power supply known as Karbon, which by now you should know, the most important of these resources would be the people who possess it.

Once again the reason why melanin beings are still curious about the origins of these organisms is for two reasons. One, they don't realize how the "spirit" of the Most High works in a physical sense, through what we call Karbon. Two, we associate the Creative force for something that would look like a human because it was said we were created in the "image of God."

Our central power source called the Sun is not just a luminary that only provides light and heat, we know that it provides life! We know that without it, life on earth would never be able to be sustained, because it is the spiritual battery keeping the matrix of Nature alive and evolving behind the artificial matrix that has captured the imagination of those who accept it. The doctrines that spring forth from their manuscripts state that one luminary would rule the day, and the other would rule the night. Because we do not use Nature to decode this message as being symbolic of the nature of the two energies inhabiting this realm, we see it as scripture relaying to us a literal description of the cosmic bodies that reside above us. The one that rules the day is also the one that rules the darkness according to "science" taught by Blancos. Is it not the Blancos who state that the source of the Moon's light is the light from the Sun, which reflects off it? So how can the Moon, even in the symbolic sense, be the ruler of the night when it is not even responsible for generating its own light?

The creation story gives the impression that these luminaries are distinct, possessing their own "light" as well as ruling independent of each other. It also gives the believer the impression that these are mere decorations in the sky as humans established themselves as the center of God's attention. Not to mention, the creation story also leaves one with the impression as if it started on day one and ended on day seven, when we know that this is an inexplicable system put into play that continues to create, evolve, and then renew itself according to the cycle of life.

So, when God said, "Let there be light" in Genesis 1:3 NIV, you cannot just interpret this is as a "light" that casts out the darkness allowing God to do the work the Sun is credited for in Nature's reality. Being reduced to just a "light" and articulating it as God's spirit in subsequent verses that is giving life to vegetation causes melanin beings to oversimplify the purpose of *their Sun.* The Sun's role is marginalized in the Bible for all the obvious reasons, when in Nature its role is indispensable to all of creation.

As I stated earlier, because we have been trained to accept God as a more powerful version of humans, we ignore what is hidden in plain sight. If the Sun is responsible for life on earth, then is the Sun itself not "alive"? Are not plants and trees alive? The difference is because they have no arms, legs, heart, brain, and lungs, we don't recognize them as life as we know it. This is why in sci-fi movies and cartoons, they have to make these trees, celestial bodies as well as animals anthropomorphic, or possessing human characteristics, for us to appreciate the beauty they possess.

You can take *any* of their "gods" away and still have life, yet if you take the Sun and the Moon away, life will cease to exist. The point is, when we see these celestial bodies as Creators, then the question will not be *who* but *what* created these organisms. This is why these Blancos recognize the Moon's energy as a power source. This source is an extremely unstable source of energy. This is why they have so many "phases" of the Moon.

If you think this is a stretch, then I dare you to refute where the term "lunacy" comes from. It is derived from the Moon's energy, and one who is full of the Moon's energy is called a "lunatic." I challenge anyone to look at one zombie, vampire, or horror movie by the Blancos and claim that you did not see the Moon snuck in there somewhere.

As Joseph Campbell had pointed out, as well as many others, the world is ruled by signs and symbols and the masses remain "symbol illiterate." The United States went even further to place its flag on the Moon, symbolizing the leadership role in eliminating the solar people of this so-called planet. Really consider how deep this con goes. Blanco "science" makes it seem that the Sun didn't have the power to create you, but it has the power to sustain you.

When you are born, your life is measured in revolutions around the Sun. You are given skin or a vessel that is designed to absorb the radiation from the Sun, so you can receive the vitamin D to make strong bones, because without strong bones you cannot make healthy blood as the blood is made in the bone marrow. When there is no more Sunlight, a signal is sent down the retinohypothalamic track, which is involved in your circadian rhythm to let the body know it is time to rest. You also know this as part of your biological clock.

Do you think it is by chance that you are supposed to be awake when the Sun is in your presence, and sleep when it is not? Furthermore, what type of world would you be living in if aspects of the Sun's spectrum were not manipulated? How do you think your radios, television images, cell phones, and X-ray machines from hospitals become a reality?

So, the question is, why is it so easy to see the Sun as the celestial body that is invaluable in keeping you alive, and not the celestial body that is the reason you are alive in the first place? When you look at the journey of the "chosen people" according to a very popular manuscript, it started over in the "Fertile Crescent," which is also a reference to the Moon. The way the land is shaped literally resembles the crescent Moon. The Fertile Crescent includes modern-day southern Iraq, Syria, Jordan, Israel, Lebanon, parts of Turkey, Iran, and Palestine.

The most ancient civilizations, including the Sumerians, were said to have started in the Fertile Crescent. The Sumerians worshipped the Moon goddess Inanna, she was called "Sin" by the Akkadians and was "Ishtar" to the Assyrians and the Babylonians. Her two main places of worship were "Ur" in the south of Mesopotamia and "Harran" to the north. The Moon god Sin was also worshipped in Saudi Arabia.

Hopefully now you see the reason why this land that we find ourselves in as melanin beings, is referred to as "modern-day Babylon!" You may have always associated that term with people who led a hedonistic lifestyle, but you failed to realize these people were intimately connected to the Moon's energy and keenly aware they are fundamentally opposed to the Sun's energy. So once again, it is not so much as *who* created them, as much as it is *what* created them.

When you refuse a human as the image of God, then the Most High will effortlessly be made known to you. We are all aware of the Moors and the impact they had on "European culture," although I have always detested entertaining conversations that center on desiring credit for bringing "European culture" to its apex, simply because when you look at the end result, melanin beings are facing extinction as well as every other "organic" being on this so-called planet.

Because this is the case, what is there to take credit for? If the idea was to take credit for civilizing Blancos, and yet they are far from civilized, what do we gain from making such an assertion? We know they are wiping out everything naturally containing the spirit of Nature in the form of Karbon, so then the only role befitting us in this narrative they articulate as the "sixth wave of extinction" is one as an accomplice to murder.

We must know that the *greatest* lie ever told to melanin beings was the slavery narrative, which was designed to discourage any thoughts that would incite a regal attitude, an attitude indispensable in elevating the melanin being to godlike status. If you were taught that you were descendants of slaves, then the next level by default would be one that merely desires to be equal. On the contrary, if our children were taught that they were the descendants of kings and queens, then the next level would only encourage them to be demigods.

Look at the sociopolitical landscape as we know it; is it not riddled with individuals all throughout the spectrum from the extreme left to the devout revolutionary, pushing for equality instead of awareness? Instead of waking up the sleeping giant, they are begging the "elite" as well as their minions who do their dirty work, to see them as equals. They rant and rave, oftentimes eloquently as to why we deserve to be treated fairly and in an equitable fashion, even though it is contrary to Nature's design.

Is it possible for your child to walk up to his friend's parents and demand that he be treated the same way as they treat their own son or daughter? If you have lived long enough and have been in many Black communities, there has been more than one occasion where you have run into someone who reminds you of a cousin, aunt, or uncle, the very reason why we choose to call perfect strangers our "brothas and sistas."

Conversely, this is the same modus operandi present within the Blanco system, albeit without the swag and appeal of melanin-rich people, but you get the point. It is also pointless to argue that Blancos fight among themselves as well, which is how many Blacks justify the division among melanin-rich beings. The only course that you are taking is one that shows how biased Nature can be. Even if there is a conflict within your own race, and it involves a brother or sister that you are related to by blood, most people would never allow harm to come to that person in front of them, whether they are right or wrong.

Because we are aware of these intrinsic qualities that Nature has instilled in us, why do we push and pull the system to produce something Nature is incapable of instituting? Considering that the energy from the Blancos is more volatile and unstable, the rule can be bent, although to keep it from breaking, the Blancos have understood what measures would need to be taken so as to prevent its race from cannibalizing itself. They understood that if the threat could be made greater from the outside than the threat that they face within, the likelihood of survival increases exponentially.

So, the subjugation of other groups of people is indeed a necessity for mental health among these organisms, which makes the journey to an egalitarian society an exercise in futility. For example, without even using melanin beings as a focal point, most movies that are made by Blancos detailing the advent of an alien invasion usually have a plot where the aliens make it to earth only to find that the inhabitants are weak and undeserving of the planet's resources, so they use their advanced technology to exterminate the less-evolved race to take over and not to coexist.

Two very important messages come from this, one is that the Blancos have made it appear that this is not *exactly* what they are doing, as well as proving the aforementioned hypothesis that power uses an outside threat to galvanize its energy. It goes to show how far gone our people have become when we can watch a movie or a TV series where the characters try to prevent a hostile alien takeover to save humanity, when this is exactly what Mother Nature is going through with the destructive and war-driven features of this hostile creature. Surely this is indeed a case where art is imitating life.

If we are led by this line of reasoning, we understand that we are not bound by a specific location but everywhere the Sun shows its divine face. As the vanguards of this realm, there is no need to dig through hidden manuscripts, travel to remote destinations, and garner degrees to validate what is already immutable, that *Nature* has already chosen a people, a people who have been kissed by the Sun! If this is our realm or our house, every room that Blancos move into has to be seen as ours, and not as theirs, simply because they had the nerve to move around the furniture and declare it as something new.

These Blancos can debate you for years without any breaks between subjects when you position your disagreement under the umbrella of the artificial matrix, but when it is inside the confines of the boundaries that Nature has set, their argument begins to fall apart at the seams.

Let us now look at history through the lens of Nature and not Blanco bias and disillusionment and see how far it takes us. The Greek word "tropikos" translates into "belonging to a turn of the Sun at the solstice." For those who have been removed from Blanco "schools" for some time, there is a region on this so-called planet called the tropics. In the north, this zone is called the Tropic of Cancer and in the south, it's called the Tropic of Capricorn. The Tropic of Cancer extends north of the equator twenty-three and a half degrees, and the Tropic of Capricorn extends twenty-three and a half degrees south of the equator.

The reasoning for this is because twenty-three and a half degrees is the latitude north and south of the equator at which the Sun will be at its zenith or highest point directly above the equator. Any latitude over twenty-three and a half degrees, north or south, the Sun will not be at its highest point when directly above the equator. This region only has two seasons, which are known as the wet season and the dry season. The temperature is on average sixty-five degrees or higher *all year around*!

The meaning behind the names is because the Blancos claim during the time of their naming, in the June solstice, the Sun's position was in the Cancer constellation, or the constellation of the crab. The naming of the Tropic of Capricorn as logic would dictate has the same reasoning behind it as the naming of the Tropic of Cancer, because as said at the time they claim the Sun, during the winter solstice was in the Capricorn constellation of the "goat."

As we will see, according to Nature, there is more to the story. As stated earlier, we must also keep in mind that the word tropic stems from the Greek word tropikos, which means a "change of direction." In other words, the Sun appears to "turn back" to go either north or south, depending on the solstice, which when broken down means "sol" for Sun, and the other half coming from the word sistere, which means "standing still." So, during the solstices, it appears that the Sun is standing still as it heads back in the opposite direction.

Now that we know the meaning behind the "science" of our Sun's positioning, we have to look at the civilizations that sprung forth from these areas, which were and still are inundated with the Sun's *radiation*. As noted before, the arguments about whether or not the Egyptians were Black, White, or even alien hybrids no longer applies when Nature has an opportunity to enter the discussion. What we know is that no matter who or what resided in this land, the godlike molecule melanin had to be present, or *no life-form* would have been able to exist.

We often forget as we hear talk of aliens and other races of people, that no matter how sophisticated and advanced their technology was promoted as being, without the natural technology found in the skin, there would have been absolutely no way they would have been able to survive in this environment, let alone make strides and produce accomplishments that are described as one of the Seven Wonders of the World.

The Egyptians knew this, that's why Osiris was depicted as green or black, both colors excellent for absorbing radiation. Sci-fi movies and programs that we entertain echo these same sentiments, although they whitewash them. They are intended to showcase the potential given to this vessel, by giving you characters that *become* the technology and not just placing emphasis on the technology itself. Considering in these regions the Sun is present roughly twelve hours a day, how on the Most High's green earth would a people with the wrong type of melanin been able to survive? The answer is, they wouldn't.

Always keep in mind that sunscreen was not invented until 1938, which, by the way, Blancos initially referred to as "glacier cream." Even after this diabolical invention, which helps to prolong the lifespan of this invasive species, they still suffer greatly even when they are in higher latitudes, away from the intense heat or radiation, if you will. For instance, when they find themselves close to tropical regions, which they term as "subtropical," they suffer greatly.

Australia is number one in the world concerning skin cancer rates, with New Zealand and the United States following close behind, just to name a few. The northern part of Australia is in the tropical region, primarily desert, and the southwestern portion is a temperate zone, which according to Blanco "science" is between forty degrees and sixty degrees latitude. New Zealand is subtropical in the north and temperate in the south and even with sunscreen and distance from tropical regions, there is still soaring cancer rates in these regions. The Skin Cancer Foundation states that "More than 2 people die of skin cancer in the U.S. every hour!"

With this in mind, as melanin beings, is it wise to have a species in control that labels our Sun as a carcinogen, propagating the idea of it being too hot so as to justify blocking out the Sun? You must know that the naming of these latitudes was more than just to describe the position of the Sun, it was really symbolic of the nature of the species that have invaded this realm.

"The origin of the word cancer is credited to the Greek physician Hippocrates (460–370 BC), who is considered the 'Father of Medicine.' Hippocrates used the terms *carcinos* and *carcinoma* to describe non-ulcer forming and ulcer-forming tumors. In Greek, these words refer to a crab, most likely applied to the disease because the finger-like spreading projections from a cancer called to mind the shape of the crab. The Roman physician, Celsus (28–50 BC), later translated the Greek term into *cancer*, the Latin word for crab" (American Cancer Society).

Did you not notice as well that the person called the "Father of Medicine," as well as the people who would follow in his footsteps, did not have the skin or the vessel necessary to live in connection with Nature, yet they are given the authority to guide you and your family in the field of health!

The very first line of defense against the outside world is the skin or the vessel given to you by the Most High. As we have already discussed, if the skin is compromised, then the bones are compromised, and if the bones are compromised, then the blood or plasma suffers greatly as well. These inherent biases make it practically impossible to get the information that will help those who possess the godlike molecule we know as melanin, or eumelanin to be specific.

This also exposes the real reason for naming the latitude the Tropic of Cancer, because it was a region in which they were fully aware of the outcome if they stayed in the region long enough for burns to occur. This also dispels the myth that Blancos could not enter deep into the region because of the Sahara. It had more to do with the Sun not allowing them to breach the region because of the high level of radiation coming from its celestial body, as well as proving that the Most High was and is always doing the most to protect the chosen people.

Also, looking at the sand simply as a barrier between us and the Blancos is also misleading because we have already determined that the sand can be used as glass and the microchip. And if you think that our people were not aware of this Khemistry, the science itself would not have been named after the region where some of our melanin beings are from. Not to mention, they consider Egypt to be in the "Middle East," and not in Africa, where we know it is located.

Can we see now how clear this story becomes when we look at the world through the lens of Nature and not through the eyes of the Blancos? They have no choice but to associate themselves with us throughout the course of their evolution, because it's not just that the Motherland is ours; this entire realm is our responsibility.

So, if we fast forward to the idea of "Europe," we know that the country is named after a Phoenician princess known as Europa. Europa is the mother of King Minos of Crete and supposedly from the city Argos in Greece. Again, if you ask Western academia if she was a melanin being of eumelanin composition, you will get a dubious reply at best, but when you look at this question to be answered through the lens of Nature you get precisely what you are looking for. Recall, as we said, there is no such thing as sunscreen as you know it today.

Argos is a city in Greece that averages temperatures in the nineties in June and July and averages temperatures of forty-five degrees in January! The question you should ask is, "Do I think at the rate that Blancos are dying now of skin cancer that they would have been able to survive and flourish in these types of temperatures without the correct vessel?" Furthermore, the Phoenicians were an offshoot of the Canaanites according to "Blanco history," and the very people who gave the Greeks their alphabet.

The Phoenicians were a Semitic-speaking people, and Semitic is a branch of the Afroasiatic languages. The branches of the Afroasiatic tongue are Semitic, Egyptian, Cushitic, Chadic, and Berber. The branch known as the Semitic languages include *Hebrew*, Aramaic, Arabic, as well as Phoenician, the language in question, among others. This also proves as a people that we should not get so caught up in thinking Hebrew is the oldest language, considering that it is a branch connected to another branch of the Afroasiatic tree.

This evidence proves that not only should all of Europe be called into question, but the origins of the so-called Greeks, considered the progenitors of Western civilization, and the precursor to the Roman empire as well. Recall, as we stated before, the origin of the Blancos is not in question in terms of the perennial stages of their development in regard to its connection to melanin beings, rather how long we were involved in the maturation process of Western culture.

The Blancos have been successful at reducing eumelanin skin to just a physical trait and not a source of power that allows for maximal absorption of light, that is, radiation, has been the closing act of these wayward magicians.

When you turn your attention to the American colonies, the lie becomes even more pronounced for all the obvious reasons indeed.

"Colonial America was overwhelmingly rural, and its few urban centers were small by European standards. The first federal census of 1790 counted only five cities with more than 10,000 inhabitants: New York City (33,000), Boston (18,000), Philadelphia (16,000), Charleston (16,000), and Baltimore (13,000). Their combined population amounted to less than 3 percent of the nation's population" (Faragher, 1998, 157).

The thirteen colonies were no bigger than counties and yet the melanin mind will imagine these settlements as the cities and states as they exist now, making the "peculiar institution" of slavery a lot larger than what it actually was. The great Dr. John Henrik Clarke repeatedly reminded us of the importance of dates, and it is through this method of reconstructing history that we will be able to make sense of a story that is full of half-truths and outright fallacies in order to complete an agenda thousands of years in the making. For instance, up to the *late* eighteenth century, cotton was a limited cash crop until the invention of the cotton gin by Eli Whitney (for the adept historians we know that these Blancos didn't invent anything unless you count lies as a tangible asset). The cotton gin, nonetheless, was invented in 1793. It was a "machine invented by Eli Whitney to remove seeds from short-staple cotton. Americans planted Sea Island, or long-staple, cotton along the Carolina coast as early as 1767" (Faragher, 1998, 214).

It goes on further to note that

"the plantation system, which appeared to be declining, was revived, with concentrations of large numbers of slaves in the hands of a few owners. Cotton exports rose from 9,840 pounds in 1789–90 to 8 million pounds in 1800–01 . . . by the 1820s the United States was the dominant world supplier of cotton, largely because of the invention of the cotton gin." (Faragher, 1998, 215).

The first question that should come to mind when you add up the numbers that have already been given is this: If America was overwhelmingly rural, with the biggest city being New York City at 33,000, how vast was this "peculiar institution" of slavery? The biggest problem with the slavery narrative is that the South was propagated as the epicenter of this crime against humanity but yet it only had a population of 16,000 in Charleston, South Carolina, which was seen as the capital of what has been deemed the "peculiar institution."

Are you trying to get me to believe that since the very first settlement of Jamestown, Virginia, in 1607, slaves on average were only picking an average of 10,000 pounds of cotton per year?! As you can tell, I am being very generous, considering that it was only a little over 100 English settlers who landed in the New World, which most died because they were a vector species who were sent to spread disease and not establish a new way of life in a strange land.

There is a reason why they would not keep track of the indigenous people of this land, because as a famous rapper, Jay Z, once said, "Men lie, women lie, numbers don't." This is a land that was plagued by wars, ravaged by disease, and stolen by contracts that were not worth the paper they were written on. The biggest variable that needs to be acknowledged is the cotton itself. As noted, the short-staple cotton was preferred but was not worth the effort put forth because extracting the seeds in the fiber proved to be too time-consuming and arduous.

So, the commodity that was central to the slavery narrative was not produced in the millions until the invention of the cotton gin? Recall, as we said, that we come closer to clarity when we use specificity rather than generalization. Short-staple cotton was preferred but grew in the *interior* of the continent, not on the shore. So why did it take so long to gain access to the interior so that they could get the more desirable short-staple cotton and not the long-staple cotton that was near the coasts?

The reason for this was the Proclamation Line of 1763, a boundary marked by the British along the Appalachian Mountains, which would prohibit the colonists from moving westward to lands occupied by "Indians" and frequented by the French, following the French and Indian War. One must remember the sly and deceptive nature of the Blancos, their historians give the reader the impression that the French and Indian War was a war between the French and the Indians, but the French and Indian War was a war between the French and the British with "Indians" fighting as allies on both sides.

After the seven-year war, the Proclamation Line of 1763 was put into action. You must remember that France's empire was vast inside the interior of the continent. They also were a more virulent vector species. As France was weakened from wars with the British and wars with the indigenous (specifically the war with Haiti), they were forced to sell 828,000 square miles of territory called Louisiana.

As we have said, rid yourself of the anachronistic mindset, envisioning Louisiana as you know it now. It was a territory, not a state at the time. To give you an idea of how vast the area was, it included fifteen present US states and two Canadian provinces! All of Arkansas, Missouri, Iowa, Oklahoma, Nebraska, and parts of North Dakota and South Dakota, to name a few. Imagine, if you will, if the French never sold their territory to the US. How big of an institution would you think slavery would have been?

The Adams-Onis Treaty of 1819 involved Spain ceding Florida to the United States or what was considered the

United States at the time, because, again, how can it be the United States as we know it when most of the states, especially in the west were not even in the possession of the United States as you know them today!

Remember what Martin Luther King Jr. said, that the difficulty in deciphering the spells are painstaking because the keys are "couched in the language." So just as Louisiana was not just a state, Florida was not just a state either, but a territory mainly occupied by "Indians" and "runaway slaves." From the story they tell us, somewhere between 1816 and 1818, right about the time of the Adams-Onis Treaty, the "United States" went into Florida to recapture "runaway slaves."

What's interesting to note is that this is right after the War of 1812. Once again, pay attention to how sly the devil can be. The War of 1812 gives the impression to the reader as if the war was only a year, when the war lasted for approximately three years. The reason why they marginalized this war is because this is a war between the British and the colonies, once again, a war where the British burned down the White House! Even as shocking as that act may seem, that is not the reason as to why the War of 1812 is not really discussed in history classes.

The reason why it is not of paramount concern to Blanco historians is because they push the date of 1776, the year they claim America proclaimed its independence from the British, yet not even forty years later they are back at war with the British, who pull out, not because they will potentially suffer defeat, but because they are at war with Napoleon, who they will eventually defeat at the Battle of Waterloo in 1815. It is the same reason Napoleon had to sell France's territory in America, because France was being stretched thin by being at war with Britain as well as dealing with the uprising in Haiti.

So, as we go back to the Seminole Wars, we are told that the reason for the first war was because they came to recapture runaway slaves, which is odd because they make it seem as if the runaways and the Seminoles were two different ethnic groups, even though they will admit that the "slaves" and the Seminoles intermingled and increased in population from doing so. See what we say about half truths!

First, and most important, when we look at this through the eyes of Nature, we realize that whomever melanin people choose to procreate with, those offspring will exhibit phenotypes that will definitely lean toward those of the dominant eumelanin expression, Second, and almost as equally as important, is the name of the "Indians" they chose to war against, who they referred to as "Seminoles," which literally means "runaway!"

So, if Florida was ruled by the Spanish and the Seminoles were considered free, why would they be given the name Seminole when they were not runaways to begin with? Also, if all of them are considered runaways, how are they to determine which ones had absconded from a life of servitude? Some historians date the Seminole Wars from 1816 to 1858, which is by far the longest and most expensive war against "Indians" in US history! So are we to believe that the US took part in a war for over forty years just because they wanted a few slaves back?! After forty years any "slave" who was on the list to be recaptured would have been too old to be of any use or may have possibly died in the conflict, not to mention according to Blanco historians, the cotton gin was the reason for the boom in cotton production, not the "slaves," so the question remains. Who were they really at war with?

Also, who in their right mind engages in a war where the costs outweigh the profits? I will tell you who they were at war with, they were at war with our people, just as they remain at war with us today! Movies based on actual events, like *Rosewood,* are reflective of the *real* conflicts that took place ever since this violent creature stepped foot on this land. As always, this feat could have never been accomplished if there were not other melanin beings who would choose to fight alongside the Blancos to make all this a reality.

It is the same problem melanin beings find ourselves confronted with today. We have always said that our biggest threat to melanin solidarity comes from the inside out. You should already know by now that there is nothing new under our Sun.

As stated before, the biggest lie ever told to us that we have accepted, is this idea we were slaves, and not warriors who fought bravely to preserve what we were entitled to by birth.

Last, but not least, if these melanin beings were "runaway slaves," as history would lead us to believe, why didn't they head north for freedom instead of south with other "Seminoles" or other "runaways," if you will. See how clear the picture becomes when you focus on the dates, discarding the method of analyzing history through the lens of compartmentalized information.

We must understand that it is not just about reading every book you can get your hands on. It is more about reading comprehension, because "if you cannot understand what you have read, then you, sir, cannot read." You must know that this reduced version of ourselves is the wall between us and the door that gives us access to the realm of our full potential. To further complicate matters, we *only* view the cotton in terms of clothing, but never realized why cotton was chosen as the fabric of choice for Blancos. If you are familiar with the flow of this manuscript, then you may have guessed right, the reason they chose cotton was because cotton was great at absorbing the Sun's radiation, with a Khemical makeup of mostly oxygen, hydrogen, and Karbon!

Karbon represents about 45 percent of the Khemical makeup of cotton, as we must remember, there is no such thing as sunscreen at this time, so the clothes they wore were essential to protecting the skin they were born with. You must understand that any problem encountered in this realm must be seen through the lens of Khemistry in order to give birth to viable solutions.

Let's go one foot deeper in the grave these liars have dug for themselves to show you just how committed they are to the lie. In 1816, Robert Finley founded the American Colonization Society which encouraged the migration of free Blacks back to the continent of Africa. One of the reasons cited as to why Blancos wanted free Blacks to go back to Africa was because after the Revolutionary War, the number of free Blacks skyrocketed into the hundreds of thousands, and these Blancos suggested that Blacks would never feel like citizens in this country, coupled with the knowledge that Blancos did not want to foster an environment where intermingling would take place and result in producing offspring with those who they considered racially inferior.

Out of the "millions of slaves," only a few thousand would emigrate between the period of 1821–1847 to what would eventually become Liberia. Even Quakers got in on the act, creating the Quaker's Young Men's Colonization Society of Pennsylvania. The vast majority of those who left on this suicide mission died due to disease and from unceasing conflicts with the indigenous in the region.

The problem with this story lies in the dates. Is it just by chance that Robert Finley created the American Colonization Society during the time when the colonists received Florida from Spain? They claim that after the Revolutionary War, there were a lot more "free slaves," but what's worth mentioning is that the colonists were not even free, going back to war with Britain in the War of 1812.

So, the question is, "How can you offer freedom to a group of people, and you are not even free yourselves!?" As history tells it, the plan of Andrew Jackson along with his "Indian allies," was to ruthlessly hunt down "runaway slaves" in the Florida territory to bring them back into slavery, but the ultimate goal was to catch as many melanin beings as possible to send them to Africa to spread Christianity, because mental chains are a hundred times stronger than physical ones.

Also, we know that Blancos have a hard time reproducing by themselves, so I think it's safe to say that by 1821 their population did not double or triple in size. Recall, the census taken in 1790 revealed that the largest city was New York with a population of only 33,000. We must come to the unsettling and uncomfortable conclusion that our own people assisted in this takeover, because with small numbers and no knowledge of the territories that are even chronicled by Blanco historians as being under the rule of the French, British, and Spanish "empires," the likelihood of them successfully maneuvering through uncharted territory is impossible, to say the least. Not to mention the weapons available to the Blancos were not as powerful and intimidating as one might believe.

In the seventeenth century, they were using a gun called the flintlock, which could do damage but oftentimes would not even kill the intended target. Before that it was the matchlock pistol, which was even worse, and the Colt revolver was not invented until the 1830s.

So, the Blancos' primary weapon, just as it is today, is that of biological warfare.

Would you not run from a being who has rabid dogs and spreads disease and has whole villages dropping like flies? So, they want us to believe that with their small numbers, very little land in their control, and useless weapons (besides disease and rabid dogs), that they were able to successfully enslave *millions* of "Africans." We even tend to give them credit in areas where they don't deserve it. We think that they were great seafarers and masters of the ocean, but out of the four voyages that the so-called Columbus was said to have taken, he crashed nine ships! Considering that the British became the premier ruler of the seas, it might be best to start there.

"The British landed in India in Surat on August 24, 1608. While India has a rich and recorded history going back 4000 years to the Indus Valley Civilisation in Harappa and Mohenjo-Daro, Britain had no indigenous written language until the 9th century almost 3000 years after India" (*India Today* Web Desk, 2019).

Historians will once again feign ignorance as to how the British were able to take over India, always pointing toward their weapons, but we have already established the most powerful weapons that Blancos had and continue to have at their disposal, and the weapons are more so of the biological and chemical variety than mechanical.

The British East India Company developed a colony called Calcutta, which served as the capital of their corporation in India.

"The British created a vast overseas empire through their supremacy over the high seas. In their colonial enterprise they were ably assisted by the Wadia ship-builders of Bombay (old spellings are advisedly used) who, drawing on their own skills, local tradition and the raw material available, provided the British navy and merchants with excellent ships" (Kochhar, 2008).

They would use these ships to bring disease and drugs to other nations to destabilize them. There is no greater example of this than the Opium Wars, the first in 1839–1842, in which Britain fought the Qing dynasty, because they refused to open up their ports to allow the British to sell opium to their people.

In the second Opium War, 1856–1860, France joined the British in their campaign to force China to open up its ports, which resulted in a ninety-nine-year lease of territories in the area, most notably Hong Kong. So, in a nutshell, because China did not want the British selling their people opium, the British went to war with them and forced them to open up their ports for trade, eventually leading to an agreement that would stand from 1898 to 1997, which inevitably led to the fall of the Qing dynasty.

The point is, is that the colonists and other Blanco empires (that is, France, Spain, Portugal) were easily defeated by the British because of their dominance of the high seas. This technology, which gave the British the advantage, was not going to be shared with the same people the British were going to war with. So because the colonists, along with other "Europeans," never possessed adequate ships and were disease ridden as well not being able to consistently travel back and forth to the Motherland because of the Sun, the only way to make progress for the world agenda being laid out, was to destabilize lands inhabited by people of color by spreading disease and pushing addictive chemicals that would zap the fighting spirit and willpower of the people.

Do we not see this same strategy playing out to this day? There have been many Blancos who have questioned the narrative and found that when they begin to try to make sense of the narrative given, it becomes practically impossible when you consider the dates and the inherent weakness of the vessel given to the Blancos by birth. One Blanco writer, in particular, boiled it down to three things, "guns, germs, and steel." This is the name of a book authored by Jared Diamond, and it shows when you are even halfway honest about the mental and physical makeup of the Blancos, you are not too far off from the conclusions that have already been drawn by most melanin scholars.

As stated before, when someone can redefine what you are, then establishing who you are becomes a piece of cake. If I can convince you that you are not a light being but a frail, emotional, and sinful human being, then it's easy to make you a Christian, Muslim, or Buddhist, etc. Let me say I am not against any of these spiritual outlooks, but I am convinced that they still lack the potential to give the clarity that is given when you entertain the reasoning given to you in the world of Khemistry.

How many movies and shows do they inundate us with to remind us that we were "slaves" and shallow thinking beings versus the shows and movies which show them as superheroes, gods, and saviors? This is the main reason why the movie *Black Panther* did so well in its debut, because not only was it refreshing to see or envision a world where melanin beings were the ones in power, we also fell in love with the idea that we could possess powers beyond what religion and academia have convinced us of.

As was stated before, the reason for all the frustration and discontent that we project on this life's experience is because we are living under the narrative written by those whom we know for certain do not and will *never* have our best interest at heart. So, when you allow someone else to write your story, then only they will be aware of the ending. This powerless position, coupled with a high level of uncertainty, is what causes melanin beings to become mentally, physically, and emotionally exhausted, until most reach the point of no return, and they become a threat to not just themselves, but to everyone around them.

Think about what we have just discussed for a second, if our history was told to us that we were warriors instead of slaves, would not the story of melanin beings building the pyramids be more believable? Even though our revolutionary thinkers have done a tremendous job in providing a mountain of evidence in support of this narrative, it remains that because we have bought, hook, line, and sinker, into the slavery narrative, it makes it practically impossible for melanin beings to truly buy into this reasoning without having any doubts or reservations.

The only way the belief in melanin beings building the pyramids could be considered true while accepting a legacy of servitude as your identity, would have been if melanin beings were seen as God's chosen people by the worlds of religion and academia, but we know that to not be the case, so we are stuck with a negative and defeatist mentality when assessing our individual and collective roles within society.

The problem is that most of us, as stated earlier, are "symbol illiterate," and cannot see that *all* of what is hidden, is hidden in plain sight. When we use this method to look for the truth, we realize immediately that one of the Blancos' best hiding places is in their language. Did you know that over half the states in the United States still have their "Indian" names? We know these names are not spelled nor phonetically expressed as they would be by the indigenous people of this land, but it remains that these beings relish the idea that they can continue to exert power over the vanguards of this realm, and they remind themselves of this power by keeping the names and events alive to remind them of this feat.

The city and state where I was born is the quintessence of this truth. Kalamazoo and Michigan are both "Indian" names, and a sculpture, which was made by Alfonso Iannelli and paid for by the YWCA, stands in downtown Bronson Park. It is a sculpture that depicts an "Indian" bowing down to a White settler. The sculpture has invoked outrage from preceding generations, but to no avail, because as we stated before, they receive and maintain power over you with such symbolism. To add insult to injury this park is downtown, right next to our court system, so imagine thinking you will receive any justice whatsoever from a system that has a symbol such as that outside of its establishment!

Nature has told us, when we look at the symbolism left by the Blancos, we will begin to understand that there will *never* be an opportunity to reconcile differences. In reality, it only leaves the melanin being with two options, remain a slave or transform into a revolutionary.

Look at the fanaticism surrounding sports in this country. Recently the name of the football team, the Washington Redskins, was changed (to Washington Football Team) because of the inflammatory and racially charged meaning behind the word redskins, as well as the history behind the term. It stands to reason if the "five-dollar Indians" were really the indigenous of this land, why would they stop there?

Look at the college teams who still possess names that are derogatory. Take the Florida State University

Seminoles, for example. We have already determined that the term "Seminole" means runaway, and that it was the longest and most expensive war fought by the United States government against the indigenous. Yet they name a "school" after this historical event? You must remember this name is a part of the "school," not just the sports teams who are a part of the institution!

Notice how when the media converses about the "higher institution," they never really mention the whole name of the "school," but when they engage in the ritual of reliving the history of the war with the natives through sports, they say the whole name! So, if there was a milestone achieved at the "school," or a tragedy, the media would just say Florida State University, but when they engage in the rituals of sports to relive the historical events, you notice they lead with the *symbol*, which would be a Seminole! The symbol is also the face of the institution in its brochures and in all its paraphernalia, which they sell to you as you express to the rest of the world that you too have now decided to participate in the ritual. These rituals, as I have said, are relived through sports!

If you are a huge fan of collegiate sports, then you know that there is a big rivalry between the states of Kansas and Missouri. Well, during the 1850s, the Jayhawks, which is the surname of University of Kansas, was also a band of guerrillas, Jayhawkers, who clashed with proslavery gangs from Missouri who were known as Bushwhackers.

The mascot for the University of Missouri is known

as "Truman the tiger," named after President Harry Truman. Truman grew up in a town ironically called Independence, Missouri, a town which was segregated as much as any town in the southern half of the "United" States. Truman was also the president who authorized the dropping of the atomic bombs in Japan in the cities of Hiroshima and Nagasaki. This mascot has won mascot of the year at least several times, and what's even more amazing is that when you watch these college games and you see the Blanco children in the stands, cheering, booing, or just being outright fanatics, you nor the rest of the gullible, never realize that they are participating in a ritual that relives history as well as reinforcing the energy that their ancestors have used to rewrite history.

Of course, we can go on and on, but I believe you get the point. So, what we have learned is that when we become symbol literate, we realize immediately that there will be no balance of power, there will be no equal footing established in this wretched matrix, only the constant reminder through symbols and in action that melanin people are enslaved, more so in the mind than with chains on the body.

This is the ultimate goal anyway, when you are from a stock (speaking of Blancos) that is numerically the minority globally. There is no way you can maintain control over the majority if there are not measures put into place to exert control over the mind. Because melanin people were and are the true natives of this realm, which would then by default make them the true natives of this land called the United States, then who better to participate in the rituals relived through sports, than us?

This is why the establishment makes the reward so great, so that we and our children literally dream of being a part of the ritual so that we can add meaning and value to our lives, all the while distancing ourselves from the gift that was given to us when we were born, not something that has to be acquired later in life by working your skin to the bone in the matrix you see in front of you.

From these revelations, one can see how ridiculous we appear when we get on our knees and pray and beg for the Most High to open up doors for us that give us full access to a system that was designed to subjugate until they could eliminate the chosen people on this so-called planet. I too suffered from the same psychosis. I felt that it was a part of my destiny to become a famous rapper and become the "nigga with the keys to the city," and leave a legacy that would be damn near impossible to eclipse.

I wrecked my brain thinking of new ways and different strategies that could be used to get me more exposure in a game that was always articulated as not being about what you know, but who you know. As I got older, I felt my window of opportunity closing in front of me and I thought, *If I were to fail at this, it would be a disastrous ending, to say the least, because I had built my whole life around this craft, indoctrinating myself with this toxic myopic outlook, because deep down I felt I was a slave to the system, and there was no other way that I and my family would be able to make it off the plantation, that is, "hood," if this did not become a reality.*

Imagine the elation and joy I would experience as slowly but surely the Most High began to awaken me from my slumber, understanding that I would have no problem seeing over the horizon as soon as I became a giant. Logic also dictates that those who become giants shall have no problem looking over clouds of despair, because when becoming a giant, you can't help but look down and realize that you are "standing on the shoulders of giants." As we take a look at hip hop and where it is today, there is no doubt in my mind that with my mindset and core set of beliefs, there would have been no way I would acquiesce and bend to the will of a sadistic, insidious, and perversion-driven cult, hell-bent on feminizing and corrupting our Black boys before they could become Black men. The same goes for melanin-rich women as well.

Do we not all remember the story of Sarah Baartman? She was a part of an indigenous tribe called the Khoikhoi, who are tied to the region of southwestern Africa. What is also amazing to note is that when you look up the description of these people, there are a few sources that show you images of a people who were lighter in complexion than Sarah herself. It is also a shame to note, just as in our situation, we shall never be aware of who she really was because Sarah Baartman is the name they gave her, not the name she was born with. They nicknamed her the "Hottentot Venus," and "Hottentot" is considered an offensive term to the Khoi people.

Venus, we all know, is the Roman goddess of love and fertility, while even the name Sarah is Hebrew, which means princess or a woman of authority and value. We must commit to memory as well that the Roman goddess Venus was the name they chose to represent the Greek god Aphrodite, who in turn was a copy and paste of the Egyptian goddesses Hathor and Isis.

Do you see now the importance of changing the names? These thieves know it gives the reader the impression that concepts and deities that were stolen were the original thoughts and ideas of these hideous warmongers. A barbarian by the name of Alexander Dunlop forced Baartman on display in the *Egyptian Hall* of Piccadilly Circus in November 1810. Again, if the Blancos were not aware of who the Egyptians were, why would they associate "Sarah" with Isis, give her a name linked to Hebrew, which is a language with roots in the Metu Neter or hieroglyphs, and then display her in an Egyptian setting? The reason is because they know damn well who and what you are!

Some historians claim she died at twenty-five, others say forty, but what we do know is she died from *disease*! When she died in 1815, they cut her body up and put it on display and continued to do so until March 6, 2002! With so many diseases plaguing the Blancos, they didn't know whether she died of syphilis, smallpox, or pneumonia, but one thing we do know is it confirms two assertions that were made earlier. One, is that they know *exactly* what and who you are. Second, is that these Blancos are a vector species spreading disease and destruction everywhere they go!

If Africa and melanin beings are the face of disease as they make it out to be today, why was she not the one spreading disease to the Blancos? It took her to be around savages to succumb to illnesses, which have already been substantiated as diseases that were and still are endemic to "European populations."

Once again, do you see how much closer you come to the truth when you use specificity instead of generalization to garner clarity? Most people who know of the story of Sarah Baartman choose to remain on the surface level regarding this tragedy, while letting so many truths escape that have remained couched in the language.

When you fast forward to the twenty-first century and look at what has happened in 2021, the United States government has decided to make Juneteenth a national holiday. As we have already discussed, we must make sure we remain symbol literate. From the evidence that has already been given, one can only conclude that this is another attempt at making sure that melanin beings *always* define their identity as a people, as those who were slaves and nothing more.

Furthermore, if we are to buy into the slavery narrative, Blancos speak of slavery one-dimensionally, as if the "peculiar institution" was just about working for free, not the exploitation of the sexual and reproductive power of melanin beings nor the wholesale theft of cultural contributions and nuances that establishes the identity of a people. When you take a look at our achievements in Africa and all across the so-called planet, would you not make a concerted effort to remain in close proximity to such a quickly evolving species?

Why is it that no matter what area of life activity you bring up, melanin beings are brought into the discussion? When Blancos bring up politics, sex, religion, entertainment, law, etc., Black people always seem to enter into the discussion, yet when Black folks get together, unless the news is trending, we seem to only be concerned with ourselves for the most part. It is only because Blancos have forced themselves into our way of life that we find ourselves compelled to bring them up.

This is why Blancos know that they can deal in political affairs on a local, national, and global level without any interference from us. It's because it is hard for us to pay attention to any other people other than ourselves! Karbon loves to bond with Karbon! Once again, it must be committed to memory why it is so important for you to *only* identify yourselves as slaves and nothing more.

Ask Blancos, "Where did Black people come from?" They will tell you from Africa, but they will only admit that when you include slavery in the narrative. If you were to ask Blancos what were melanin beings doing before they were enslaved, you will get a dubious response at best. Since time began, somehow they say, you were in Africa this whole time and never knew that aliens were building pyramids and huge monuments all around you! If anyone had known of aliens or any group of people for that matter, building the pyramids, would it not have been you and your people? Or were we too busy living in jungles fighting lions and chucking spears at one another for us not to notice greatness being immortalized in stone all around us?

Even if Blancos have convinced you that it was not your people who built the pyramids, we know that our people had eyes and could see who did! Therein lies the strength of the slavery narrative, it gets our people so emotional that we overlook the details and go right into the pain and suffering and the horrible circumstances that had to be endured in order to make it to the "mountaintop." If the Blancos were so concerned with the truth, why is it in their "schools" you read the introduction and then end up skipping chapters that they will pick up on in college if you happen to be eager enough to pursue a career and maybe figure out more of the story that is hidden in plain sight.

Even on the collegiate level, you will skip chapters and discuss and debate topics that the institution via the professor chooses to indoctrinate you with. Then you wonder why the Blancos and other races of people, including melanin beings, have no answers to life's mysteries. How can you ever engage life with a holistic approach when you wallow in the mud of compartmentalized information?

I will give you a great example of how this works. During

and after the 2020 presidential election, there were worries of voter fraud and corruption at the highest level, culminating in what would be called a "storm on the capital." Every news outlet was either defending the integrity of the election process or encouraging anarchy by suggesting there were voting irregularities that would cause Trump to lose the election, never mind that Trump lost the popular vote in 2016 but won the electoral college.

Regardless of what position was taken, both platforms had a common denominator. Both feigned ignorance of the corruption that is inherent in the design of the system. What needs to be highlighted more than any other episode in political theatre is the election of 1824. In 1824, John Quincy Adams was running against Andrew Jackson and something very unique happened, which if touched upon, would have sent shockwaves through the world of political pundits and experts as well as the racist dummies who hang on their every word.

In 1824, Andrew Jackson won the *electoral college and the popular vote, and he still lost!* In the election, Andrew Jackson won a plurality of both the popular vote and electoral vote, but when it was sent to the House of Representatives for a recount, John Quincy Adams was declared the winner! This is how things were working out for a while, the "leader" being chosen by a selected few, this period of time was called the Era of Good Feelings.

You must know that the first nine presidents were under a one-party system, known as the Republican-Federalists.

As I have stated earlier, this is all political theatre, because if we fast forward to the 2016 election with Hillary Clinton and Donald Trump, if Hillary had hated Trump as much as Trump hated her, which she had a right to with all the empty rhetoric by Trump claiming he would throw her in jail if he were to get elected to office, then Hillary would have fought tooth and nail to at least declare to the public that she won the popular vote, and declared just as Trump declared, the people have chosen, and yet not even as much as a whisper came from that degenerate.

Neither did Andrew Jackson fuss or fight with the way things had played out, because he would be elected or, excuse me, selected as president the very next term in 1828. So, what I am saying to you, is why should I listen to a group of savages when they claim they know the history of melanin beings, yet they prove time and time again that they are not even aware of their own?!

Once again, we have been trained to become emotional and to respond more like a reactionary than a revolutionary. For instance, 1850 to 1950 was the period in which the most popular form of entertainment was minstrel shows, a form of entertainment where Blancos would paint their faces black and parade around as caricatures of melanin beings. If one peers deeply into this disturbing practice, you realize that it says more about the insecurities that are embedded in their mental disposition, than it does about putting forth an effort to dehumanize and ridicule the Most

High's chosen people. Mark Twain, a famous American writer, propagated as "the greatest humorist this country [the United States] has produced" (*New York Times,* 1910), said on more than one occasion that he absolutely loved minstrel shows. If melanin beings were to hear this, they would automatically conclude that Mark Twain was a racist and possessed a hatred for those who were blessed with the black/brown combination of melanin.

This quote from Mark Twain, while he was in India for a festival, will show you the ambivalence that exists in the mind of the Blancos, which may be seen as hatred to us, but envy in the eyes of Nature. As Twain was enjoying the festival, he wrote,

"I could have wished to start a rival exhibition there, of Christian hats and clothes. I would have cleared one side of the room of its Indian splendors and repacked the space with Christians drawn from America, England, and the Colonies, dressed in the hats and habits of now, and of twenty and forty and fifty years ago. It would have been a hideous exhibition, a thoroughly devilish spectacle. Then there would have been the added disadvantage of the white complexion. It is not an unbearably unpleasant complexion when it keeps to itself, but when it comes into competition with masses of brown and black the fact is betrayed that it is endurable only because we are used to it. Nearly all black and brown skins are beautiful, but a beautiful white skin is rare" (Twain, 1890, 222).

So, what we learn is that those who appear to hate those who possess the black/brown combination of melanin do so because they realize they are not at odds with the people who have been shown favor by Nature, but actually at odds with Mother Nature herself. We receive the brunt of this contention because we are the only ones who can respond in a way where they can receive feedback from Mother Nature, because we personify Mother Nature's energy.

Melanin beings become arrogant and assume it is just us who are subject to the cruelty of these savages. But name any corner of the earth that is not in danger of collapse because of gross negligence and greed. Name one animal possessing Karbon that is not in danger of becoming extinct because of the desire to exploit Nature, coupled with the inherent desire to kill anything that presents a challenge to their perceived dominance over Nature.

Recall, if you will, throughout your life's learning experience about the Blancos and their relationship with Mother Earth. They use terms like dominate, control, and conquer, while melanin beings use terms like share, coexist, and balance. Now that the Blancos have spun the world out of control, the excuse is that there are too many people on the planet, too many resources being used up, too much instability within ecosystems, which breeds disease and famine, but none of these things were an issue while the building and expanding of their empire was in play.

For all those who may be reading this book and of are another persuasion, this is not to convince you of anything, because whether you would like to admit it or not, you already know the truth. When savage and chaotic behavior is in the ruler's position, destruction and turmoil do not lag far behind. This is not a question of *if*, but rather *when* these things will happen. Those in power are aware of the power of our Sun but refuse to admit that the vessel that they have been outfitted with possesses energy that is diametrically opposed to the energy that comes from the central power source we call the Sun.

In roughly twenty states in the US, it is illegal for any Blanco person under the age of eighteen to patronize tanning salons. Now you have to think, even if their children are not aware of the dangers that come from artificial sunlight, what do you think those in power know about natural sunlight? They pass legislation to protect their young, because they know that ignorance is not bliss. This is why discussions with those who claim to not be racist and profess to treat everyone the same are of no concern, because melanin beings know that they are not the ones in power, and the ones in power are the captains of the ship.

These savage beings are well aware of the Khemical makeup of this realm, and realize that no matter how anyone feels, Nature has rules, rules that must be obeyed in order to maintain balance and aa viable future for the

Karbon universe. I want you to think critically about our state of affairs for a second. From what we are told, we are dealing with a being who has built skyscrapers to tower over cities, submarines to navigate the depths of the oceans, telecommunication networks that allow businesses as well as the common person to communicate instantly thousands of miles apart, and rocket ships that travel to outer space in an effort to find new life, although they have done a horrible job of respecting the life-forms that exist on this so-called planet, but they have done all these things, and yet they still cannot curb their enthusiasm for killing melanin beings.

You would think with all the godlike tasks the Blancos have taken up, they act like treating people with dignity and respect requires a herculean effort. They put panels together, form coalitions, consult social and political scientists, all to figure out what measures can be taken to ensure that everyone has an opportunity to pursue happiness. How can a people who have labeled themselves "conquistadors" convince the world that one day the lion will lie down with the sheep? How can we trust beings who go in their lab under the guise that they are there to find cures and push past the limits of human imagination, yet it seems the only thing that comes from these labs in remote facilities are biological and chemical weapons, which always seem to find themselves directed at people with the black/brown combination of melanin?

Everything about us was seen as backward and primitive

when looked at through the eyes of the Blancos, but when looking at life through the eyes of Nature, everything makes perfect sense. You see tribes in Africa wearing little to no clothing and think that these people are backward or lagging behind in how the world works, because of course the Blancos have made a huge industry out of clothing and branding this clothing and calling it fashion. Although when the melanin beings look at life through the lens of Nature, they begin to realize Nature had gifted them with a vessel that was designed to absorb as much of the radiation from the central power source we call the Sun, with the intention of giving them every opportunity to become a facilitator of the highest level of spiritual expression that can only come about through the absorption of light.

Dr. Kamau Kambon, a wise man, said, "The first one to the mind is the winner" (Kambon, no date). Melanin goddesses have allowed their frustration to boil over when they attempt to understand why the melanin kings they birth out do not return the love and respect to them and all melanin queens who are an extension and reflection of that powerful energy given them by Mother Nature. Before I give the reasoning behind this, I will state emphatically that I take no sides, but rather use a sensitive issue to highlight a process that is overlooked but extremely important in making sure the division continues and the goal is achieved.

We must remember that even though work and school are propagated as roads leading to adulthood, they are also places that create opportunities for romantic relationships as well as defining and adhering to roles given by people in position of authority. In one or both of these settings, most, if not all, people have cultivated intimate relationships with others of the opposite or same gender. What is often overlooked, and sometimes completely ignored, is the perverse behavior from those in a position of authority as they engage in inappropriate relationships with students or employees who are overworked and underpaid. Even though this is egregious, this is not the point of emphasis.

The point being made here is that this exercise is one in which those who are being controlled are always made aware of their position in society. They literally call this socialization! From pre-K to middle school, 80–90 percent of the teachers are Blanco women! They rear your children as you go to work, more than likely for Blanco men. These women at these "schools" prepare your child's mind to be in service to the empire. They are fully aware that the curriculum does not resonate with the melanin beings because all they do is sit in a building where they learn about the accomplishments of Blancos. Think about it, if Blanco children had to be tested on how much they knew about Black inventors, artists, and scientists, they would be fairing just as poorly as our children are at this time.

They tell you that slavery was such a long time ago, but in the same breath, they will force you to learn about empires that existed in Greece and Rome thousands of years ago! While at work, you see pictures of Blanco men and Blanco women who hold positions of authority. They bait you with the idea that as long as you work hard and don't miss more than a few days at work, upward mobility is guaranteed somewhere in the near future. For some, this does become a reality, but at what cost?

The success of the individual is at the expense of the family! This is something well-known by the Blancos. How many commercials and ads do you see or hear that advertise businesses as family owned and operated? The Blancos are fully aware that the family who makes money together, grows together! When you work a job, you find that you become closer to your coworkers than you do with your own family. Many times this is the case, even with the family you start with the person you make a commitment to, whether it's just a long-term relationship or marriage. How often have you heard a person use the phrase, "That's my work wife," or "That's my work husband"?

They tell you to get a job to gain work experience, knowing full well that if you don't commit to that job for a number of years, it does not look good on your résumé when you start the process of looking for employment, which will pay better or offer more opportunity for growth in a field that you may be interested in. You appear to look like a bad "slave," if your work history shows that you are not willing to stick around for years at a time.

In the meantime, the Blanco woman is there to teach your son and daughter life lessons, which also by default encourages and reinforces the god complex given to her. Not only now is she the standard of beauty in the Western world, she also is a teacher and cultivator of minds, demanding that you be on your best behavior when in her presence. Because both the melanin boy and girl are in the same position, they both begin to subconsciously realize that acceptance by the Blanco woman gets them one step closer to being accepted by Western society, although we know full well this never is the case.

Since 2020, and the escalation of uncertainty in every area of life activity, we have been able to push aside the veil that stands between what we think is going on versus what is actually going on. From our children not being fed first, only being able to eat after Blanco children are fed, to the cutting off of locks just to participate in sports, as well as leaving a melanin baby in daycare *all by herself* because the staff had claimed that the baby "looked like a doll." Most parents within our community have experienced or been so upset by what they have been witnessing that they now have chosen to homeschool their children, so these sorts of traumatic experiences never get a chance to take away the little peace of mind that our children have a chance to hold on to.

Does it not seem odd to you that we are the only ones on this so-called planet who have been convinced that we should not take up the responsibility of teaching ourselves about ourselves. As long as we are taught by Blancos, we will be convinced that the world's resources are limited.

Take, for instance, the melanin King Moses, not Moses as in the biblical character, but ironically enough they have the same character. Moses is an engineer who invented a machine that can produce thousands of gallons of fresh clean water a day by extracting the water out of the air. He placed his machines in war-torn areas like Flint, Michigan, and Haiti, where melanin beings were in need, and, as expected, a few of his atmospheric machines have been sabotaged.

The crazy part is that many in the so-called conscious community have still been campaigning for the same government to get involved that caused the problems in the first place, while Moses became proactive and did something about it. The reason why it has not received a lot of coverage is because it is imperative to the agenda that scarcity is propagated at all costs, because if people feel that primary resources are limited, panic and societal breakdown is inevitable if the stuff ever hits the fan.

This is also something that was always hidden in plain sight because if you have ever had a basement flood or it's too muggy inside the house, you bring out the dehumidifier and it takes the humidity, that is, removes water from the air! We never tend to look at things in this way because we have given Blancos a seat of power in our sacred house, and that is the dwelling where the mind resides.

If the Blanco grocery stores close down, will the ground stop producing food? We know this is not the case, but, unfortunately, we have distanced ourselves from Nature so that we wouldn't know the first thing about growing our own food. This is not to say this goes for all our people, but for too many of them this is indeed the case. The Blanco life of speed and convenience has stripped the melanin beings of their drive to remain connected to the environment that gives back what you put into it.

Do you think if everyone was a farmer that the government could scare people by telling them that grocery stores were in danger of closing down? How many farmers did you see at grocery stores in a panic filling their carts to capacity with an extreme look of desperation on their faces? It has been said time and time again, that our people die from lack of knowledge.

Recall what was stated in the Preface of this book, that when we feel the need to make these things happen, we will find a way, because I firmly believe that necessity is the mother of invention. So, with that being said, when times move into the halls of desperation, we naturally invent more ways to tackle issues, which requires more time and thought to figure out than the time and effort that was put forth to bring the problem into fruition.

We have to understand the true nature of the being that we find ourselves in contrast to. Blancos are a species who are obsessed with war. The Blanco economy is intimately tied and connected to its war machine. Most people are not aware that over 60 percent of the world's weapons are sold by the United States and Russia.

Recall what war had done for the American economy

after the Great Depression. You should also commit to memory the scandal they called Operation Fast and Furious, where the Central Intelligence Agency (CIA) was exposed selling weapons to the Mexican cartels, the same cartels and gangs that became the reason Trump wanted to seal off the borders.

The question is, How can a government that continues to commit crime, ever place itself in a position to prevent crime? Remember when I had mentioned the book, *Guns, Germs, and Steel*? What should have been in the author's title was "Drugs" as well, it would have completed the picture necessary for clarity that is clear.

The grandfather of President Franklin D. Roosevelt was an opium dealer. President John F. Kennedy's father was a bootlegger. Along with giving the indigenous population disease, the Blancos made sure to give them alcohol as well, because most people tend to forget that alcohol is a drug. The Harrison Narcotics Tax Act of 1914 placed a tax on drugs like cocaine, heroin, etc., while marijuana was legal as well with a tax being placed on it in 1937. By 1970, all these drugs would be considered illegal by the United States government as President Richard Nixon began the first war on drugs.

The point I'm trying to make here is understand who you are up against, a being that will lie, cheat, steal and kill in order to maintain power. Most people were under the assumption that the legalization of marijuana is the first time this has ever happened in this country. As stated earlier, before the Harrison Narcotics Tax act of 1914, *all* drugs were considered legal, it was just a tax on these substances. This is why you had a period of time they referred to as the Roaring Twenties.

What is interesting to note is that during the 1920s, they enacted Prohibition, making alcohol illegal, yet opiates and every other hard drug under the Sun was legal. The whole point of Prohibition from the standpoint of their story was to clean up America and drop crime rates. From the evidence I am about to give, this was never the reason they banned alcohol, essentially keeping all the harder drugs legal.

So, the question remains, Why would America ban alcohol and not other illicit drugs that could and would do more damage to the American public than alcohol could ever accomplish? The problem was melanin beings were making strides and becoming an economic powerhouse in America! We often are told about Black Wall Street, but we fail to realize our people were moving past the Blancos at phenomenal speeds, creating jobs for their people, all the while selling products and providing services to Blancos, reinvesting in the Black community, causing dollars to circulate many times over before ever leaving that community and ending up back in the hands of the Blancos.

In the 1920s, we were still disproportionately affected by the laws in the racial caste system developed by the United States, but we still continued to thrive.

"In 1920, 35.2% of male prisoners were black, although they only made up 10.4% of the male population" (Waterman, 2016).

Even though this was the case, White men still made up 65 percent of the prison population at the time. When you fast forward to the twenty-first century, the numbers flip, which is mindboggling, because Black men made up and still make up a small percentage of the male population in the United States.

"In 2010, 53.6% of male prisoners were black, although they only made up 10.4% of the male population" (Waterman, 2016).

What they saw in the early twentieth century was a concerted effort by melanin beings to corner markets. In our self-made towns, we had our own doctors, lawyers, and entertainment hubs where we made our own alcohol. We were self-sufficient and desired the autonomy the Blancos claim we detest now.

An article in the *Oklahoma Historical Society* proves otherwise, and I quote,

"The All-Black towns of Oklahoma represent a unique chapter in American history. Nowhere else, neither in the Deep South nor in the Far West, did so many African American men and women come together to create, occupy, and govern their own communities. From 1865 to 1920 African Americans created more than fifty identifiable towns and set-tlements" (O'Dell, no date).

He goes on further to state,

"All-Black towns grew in Indian Territory after the Civil War when the former slaves of the Five Tribes *settled together* for mutual protection and economic security. When the United States government forced American Indians to accept individual land allotments, *most* Indian 'freedmen' chose land next to other African Americans. They created cohesive, prosperous farming communities that could sup-port businesses, schools, and churches, eventually forming towns" (O'Dell, no date), italics added.

I know it's not hard to notice why certain words are in italics, especially the part that said they "settled together." And I hope you caught that not only did these Black towns grow in "Indian territory," but that when the government was issuing land allotments to "Indians" it decided to choose land next to "African Americans."

Last but not least notice how this Blanco author said their farming communities helped to support busi-nesses, *schools*, and churches. Use your critical thinking skills: if these "Africans" and "Indians" were fresh out of slavery, how did they create these businesses, schools, and churches if "slaves" didn't know how to read? More important, if you recall when we discussed the Seminole wars, the "escaped slaves" and the "Indians" just so happened to be living together then. The only conclusion that one can draw without any doubt or reservation is that we were the damn "Indians!"

We know without a shadow of a doubt, if you settle among melanin people and offspring become a product of that union, there is no way the dominant traits of the black/brown combination of melanin would not express itself, so there is no denying that our people were a huge part of "Indian" history, even if you don't buy into the idea of us being the "Indians" ourselves. Conclusions like this become very easy to draw when we look at the world through the lens of Nature and not the reconstruction of history told to us by those who have an agenda.

The most famous town that we know of from this region, as you have already guessed, would be Tulsa, Oklahoma. And once again, how were these people becoming independent in every area of life activity if they were slow, illiterate degenerates who needed the Blancos to remain afloat? Considering that we were excellent farmers, growing marijuana and developing breweries was nothing new to the indigenous communities. In the late nineteenth century and early twentieth century, this became commonplace, as this article states.

"The burgeoning market for high-quality brews has become a trend among black-owned breweries and beer aficionados" (Ebony Mag Team, 2015).

By the mid- to late-twentieth century, the government had all but sabotaged any hopes of creating a business that would have been the source of generational wealth for decades to come.

"A man of action, [Theodore] Mack assembled a group of investors under the United Black Enterprises banner with the hopes of purchasing the Blatz brand [of beer] from Pabst [Brewing Company] in 1969 after the federal government forced its sale. Mack told reporters that UBE made its $8 million offer on 'behalf of the 22 million black people in this country'" (Tanzilo, 2016).

The article further states, they eventually came across the Peoples Brewery, which according to Blancos, was ranked tenth among the fourteen breweries in Wisconsin at the time (Tanzilo, 2016). How many of our people knew that our melanin tribes were causing headaches for the establishment, using their knowledge of Khemistry to create industries that would benefit the whole and not the individual?

These Blancos love to feign ignorance as to why such measures were taken when according to them, the measures taken made absolutely no sense at all, until you factor in the strength and power on display by melanin-rich tribes who were determined to make a way for a people who were under constant attack. We all know the saying "order out of chaos," and that is just what the doctor ordered, because to justify the expansion of government agencies, there must be an environment that creates the need for this.

"Alcohol became more dangerous to consume; crime increased and became 'organized'; the court and prison systems were stretched to the breaking point; and corruption of public officials was rampant . . . Prohibition removed a significant source of tax revenue and greatly increased government spending. It led many drinkers to switch to opium, marijuana, patent medicines, cocaine, and other dangerous substances that they would have been unlikely to encounter in the absence of Prohibition" (Thornton, 1991).

You see Hollywood or the government (I have a hard time telling the two apart), made sure that we saw Italian gangsters as the cause for all the instability, and they were the good guys just trying to make good old America safe, upholding the responsibility of moral leaders of the free world, but in reality nothing could be further from the truth. Did you also know that the US Internal Revenue Service (IRS) use to enforce Prohibition before it was a responsibility given to the US Department of Justice?

As you can see, there is no way that I can listen to Blancos tell me anything about the history of my people when I know more about their history than they do! Our resiliency is unmatched, but you would not know that because too many of us pay attention to what these liars say on their news networks and other media outlets. When we do well, especially in the face of adversity, do you think anyone would notice? The propaganda machine is so powerful, even we buy into the lies without any disagreement or contempt.

"The black middle class is booming. The number of affluent African-American families with incomes over $50,000 rose from 266,000 in 1967 to over 1 million in 1989" (Dillin, 1991).

The article goes on further to state,

"William O'Hare, head of Population and Policy Research at the Urban Research Institute, University of Louisville, was one of the report's authors. He observes: 'It's a different ballgame than it was a generation ago. For example, in 1940, 95 percent of all blacks were below the poverty level. Even in 1950 or 1960, if blacks were not poor, they had been raised in a poor family'" (Dillin, 1991).

So, as the article states, in a generation, melanin beings were determined to change things, even attaining success at the height of the acquired immunodeficiency syndrome (AIDS) and crack epidemics! We all know, though, this is not what you heard on the news via TV and radio during that era. What you heard was that we were drug dealers, rapists, and lazy bums who were being raised by "welfare queens." This propaganda worked so well that George

Bush Sr. was able to get elected to the highest office in the US by pumping these stereotypes.

Bush was running against Governor Michael Dukakis of Massachusetts, and cited the case of Willie Horton, an African American prisoner who was released on a weekend furlough program and ended up raping a White Maryland woman and stabbing her boyfriend. The ploy made Dukakis look soft on crime, and it would ignite anger and fear in an already volatile and hate-filled Blanco community. This not only gave Bush the edge in the race, it also determined criminal justice policy up to the present day.

As you can see, there has always been, and will always be, a concerted effort to demonize and vilify the people who Nature has chosen. What we have yet to understand is that *everything* in this Karbon matrix has the ability to transform. When we embrace this logic, we begin to proceed with caution, becoming fully aware that because *all* energy has the ability to transform, the lie can become the truth.

When you invest your time battling and/or embracing the images manufactured by vampires, you will begin to blame yourself, for there will be no bite marks or scars for evidence when you allow demons to feed off your thoughts. The only one left standing to blame is the reduced, yet overworked, version of you, which must now realize that it will take the real version of you to awaken the giant and recapture the imagination.

How are you preparing for a battle outside of you, if you refuse to fire one shot inside the seat of consciousness?

It's incredibly tragic that so many melanin beings place emphasis on the past and the future as if *now* never counts! Life teaches you that every experience has a birthplace, and every journey has a destination. We must use every second available to us to colonize the mind, acting swiftly in our judgment and merciless in our execution.

Why should we wait for hard times to befall us to harden our hearts? It angers the Most High to see so many melanin warriors transform their lives into a spectator sport. What have you got to lose, if you decide for the rest of your life you will never stop believing in self? The Most High can do wonders if you allow her to run this race with you, picking up the pace to speeds that give one the impression you started the race from the finish line.

This method only works when you are unwavering in your approach, cultivating perseverance in every available moment. Do not be afraid to be different. You must be if you are to tackle the issues placed in front of you. Your identity has been taken from you and repackaged and placed in sci-fi movies and television programs. They make sure they inundate you with Black death, destruction, and despair until you get to the point of exhaustion, caring more about being in your emotions and less about the eventuality. These ups and downs happen for a reason; it is part of the rebuilding process. It's safe to say in order to completely rebuild, a person must first tear down the old.

You are a people who have brought so many gifts to the world and yet have overlooked the greatest gift of all, the vessel that is endowed with energy that is endless when it is tapped into. To me, it is hypocrisy to hear the media go on and on about how weak and helpless our people are on every level, yet when you bring up the consequences of not having the vessel capable of navigating through this realm of radiation, the conversation gets quiet. But as long as the two groups are talking about weaknesses and mishaps made by melanin-rich beings, the ridicule and scorn can go on forever.

We have gotten so used to the lies, it seems as if they are the only things we can talk about. When someone presents the truth to you, it's almost as if you gravitate to it. No one has to convince, manipulate, or coerce you, because the vessel is already in awareness of how the spirit works. I used to think for a long time that life would be easier if you could literally be something or someone different, until I rediscovered myself and got reacquainted with the cosmic energy that was always residing inside of me.

I no longer cared about the superficial things in life—money, cars, and clothes—because I knew if I could just tap into my greater self all those things that I desired would be of no consequence or of any use to me. It amazes me that in my younger days, I would be so disgusted with my position, equating material possessions with success. To be honest, I was less in a rush to give praise to the Most High if I did receive those things, rather more in a rush to tell the world, "I told you so."

This drive for validation among people who were and still are lost themselves is no longer a part of my being.

I can say with confidence that the only secret in life that I ever had to figure out *was me*! When I came to this realization, thi adage (inscribe on the Temple of Apollo at Delphi) "Know thyself, and thou shalt know all the mysteries of the Gods and of the universe," began to resonate on a fundamental level (dare I say it?), a molecular level.

As Khemistry opened its doors, that happened to be closed for thousands of years, I began to feel a sense of relief that I have never felt in all the days I have been a part of this experience. I just knew in my heart of hearts, the Most High just would not make life this hard. But the way the Blancos manipulate information, I knew it would be a bit deeper than just picking up a book and reading it. I knew it would take discernment and patience but most of all commitment to an idea that would transform itself into conviction.

I remember watching a three-minute video on YouTube titled "How the Sun Sees You" (Leveritt, 2014). It was a group of scientists who went around showing people how their skin or vessel looked under an ultraviolet (UV) camera. If you were a melanin being, then your skin just absorbed the light, but if you were a Blanco, the UV camera would show the Sunspots and the blemishes in the skin. What was truly remarkable is when the scientists had the volunteers place sunscreen on their faces, and it was shocking to see that when they applied sunscreen on their faces, under a UV camera, it appeared as if they had on blackface!

It immediately made me realize, the minstrel shows were not an attempt to dress up and act out as exaggerated characters of melanin beings, as entertainer Al Jolson would sing in songs like "My Mammy." There was this cry and plea being sent to Mother Nature asking, Why would you do such a thing if my existence is to have any shot of living in harmony with you?

It made me realize the frustration felt by Mark Twain and even Blancos I knew or just happened to walk by on a summer day, showing a lot of skin, in a rush to appear as if they naturally possess the eumelanin that makes this realm so special. I realized these cries were trying to mimic the cries of the greatest masterpiece ever performed by Nature, and that is the cries that announces the arrival of the Karbon baby.

PART 3

The Vampire Living Inside You

Imagine, if you will, a warrior preparing for battle, heart racing from anticipation, war paint covering wounds from previous conflicts, wielding a sword too heavy for both hands, carrying the burden of devastating losses of those you love who were united by faith. The only force moving one leg in front of the other is the dedication and zeal for the liberation of a people who have been bathed in greatness since the waters moved to and fro in the days of antiquity.

On this day, the warrior was told this would be the war of all wars, or the war to end all wars. This revelation alone would have been enough to prepare the warrior to make the ultimate sacrifice, but the approval and guidance of the Most High have always been sufficient. His soul had set forth a path leading to the war of all wars, and it had indicated to him that it would take place at the highest elevation known to humans.

This riddle was the sole reason the warrior would travel to distant lands, scaling one mountain after another, reaching the summit only to find there was no war there, only another opportunity to look over the land and reacquaint himself with the journey. What he found even more perplexing is that every adventure undertaken and every mountain he scaled, he would hear battle cries as well as seeing the dried blood of fellow warriors who left those all too familiar patterns that war viciously scatters across decadent blades of grass.

After years of venturing, coupled with the exhaustion that only failure can bring about, he finally made it back to his homeland. In a state of despair and desperation, he drops his sword and shield where he stands and prostrates himself before the Most High and cries out and says, "I have done everything you have asked of me, so where is this battle that warriors of the distant past have proclaimed frees you from the cycle where peace is only a time where you prepare for the next war?" As he falls to his knees, he asks, "Have I not done all you have asked of me? I am beginning to think that death and tranquility are merely two faces of the same coin."

Just then, as his eyes are closed, the war cries and beating drums build in momentum, the sounds of swords clashing and men wailing are almost deafening. Almost in an instant, the warrior begins to understand that the highest mountain known to humans is his crown chakra, or the "bridge to the cosmos."

He finally understands that the war to end all wars will take place in the mind and not in any location visible to man. *How quickly tears can turn to laughter,* he thought, as he realized that no matter how many steps he takes, he is still the same distance from the final war. Finally free, his sword and shield become useless to him now, as he had come to the realization that freedom is always, and will always be, a warrior's greatest weapon.

This story should resonate with us all, as we find ourselves on our own personal journey. We must realize we can be of no real use to the struggle for liberation if we have not vanquished the enemy inside of us. Unfortunately, those in power understand this, and they also understand that the enemy they have placed inside of us possesses a duality that we must be able to identify and then eliminate if we dare to stand a chance.

This duality consists of a mindset as well as an organism that can be measured by light and behavior. At its peak, it denies any shots of upward mobility, while encouraging the devolution of the melanin being. This mindset that you have been poisoned with, coupled with the iron grip of this organism, can dramatically affect your behavior, causing you to bend to their will, prioritizing its needs over your own. The system will not stop until it consumes its host, and even after that it will consume the vessel you were given at birth, leaving no evidence of you, besides the memories kept by the ones who love you.

This two-headed beast can cause you to overreact, becoming a person who is unbearable to be around. It causes the body to become greedy and relish in gluttony. Many more heads can spring from its body, which allows the "scientific" community to call them by many names, but the end result is the same. For most, the grief appears to be foreign because death ensures the faces are different.

This mindset along with this organism has been a part of your "genome" since the dawn of this parasitic civilization, yet they both go by simple names, because in lay terms it causes you to overlook its power and significance. Let's isolate the first head of this beast, wherein a few of its cells can turn into billions overnight! The hell with all the suspense, you will now be thrust into the world of yeast, *Saccharomyces*, the sugar fungus!

The layperson may be asking, "Is fungus that big of a deal and how and why should its significance be elevated to the highest level of consideration?" Simply put, it is because it feeds on what maintains life in this world facilitated by an element we know as Karbon! We must know that the naming of things will determine how we perceive these things. This practice is called nomenclature.

To laypeople, they know it as simply sugar, but in Khemistry and more closely related disciplines, it is known as saccharides. The most well-known are monosaccharides (glucose, fructose, and galactose), disaccharides (sucrose, maltose, and lactose), and polysaccharides (cellulose, starch, and glycogen). The Karbon in each of these sugar groups is just the most well-known, but my point is to prove to you how critical Karbon is to the functions of life, not to overwhelm you with a litany of scientific jargon.

We must go through the basics, though, so you understand two things. One, how crucial Karbon is to Nature's matrix. Two, how the manipulation of Karbon is the source of all the confusion and the framework for humanmade mysteries that will conveniently enough plague "science" until they are able to manifest destiny. So, what you should know is, *mono* is one, *di* is two, and *poly* is many.

- When you add two simple sugars together, or monosaccharides, you get a disaccharide.
- When you put more Karbon together, you get a polysaccharide.
- When glucose and fructose come together, you get sucrose, which is the equivalent of table sugar.
- When you put glucose and galactose together, you get lactose.
- When you put two glucose molecules together, you get maltose.

The pattern that I hope has become evident to you is that *glucose* is the common denominator. Glucose is the most abundant simple sugar in the Karbon universe, with plants being the primary source of where this sugar comes from. Notice how the Blancos then try to confuse you and use big words to alienate you from the source of this life-giving property by calling them "carbohydrates," which is a term that identifies that its Khemical makeup is Karbon, hydrogen, and oxygen. Another way to hide it is to make it short and just call it "carbs," but either way, there is no way they can get away that we are still talking about Karbon! One must always remember Karbon is only Latin for *coal*!

The reason why glucose is extremely important is because it is the *only* fuel that the blood runs on. And we know that blood is 55 percent plasma, so the fourth state of matter chooses to only run on this fuel. The Blancos know this so well, so they manipulate the fuel for plasma and when they do, it destabilizes the human body, leading to the number one metabolic illness on the planet! You know this "disease" as diabetes!

Do you know that within the diabetic population, type 2 diabetes is the most prevalent? Type 2 is acquired from the diet and represents over 98 percent of the diabetic population! It is rare to be born with type 1 diabetes because, as we know, the Most High would never be so cruel as to create the Karbon baby with the inability to harness its energy.

This is literally Karbon bonding with Karbon, and we know through Khemistry that when Karbon bonds with Karbon, it only creates *diamond*! What this also proves is how dark and insidious this being is, because when they don't have the ability to spread the diseases that are endemic to their population, *they create them*!

We know that blood absorbs light, blood is 55 percent plasma, and blood is sacred, according to religious texts, so why do the Blancos marginalize its importance by making it seem that its main responsibility is to just deliver nutrients and rid the body of waste? Look at how they make "horror movies" that are full of "blood and gore," as they describe it, conditioning the mind to perceive it as just a "red liquid" and not the awesome and magnificent power containing the fourth state of matter!

When a person's blood sugar is low or they just have donated blood, the advice is to eat more Karbon or "carbohydrates" in order to regain energy, and because ignorance is bliss, the melanin being does not realize that their body's Khemistry is using Karbon to make more Karbon! Your plasma is unique to you, even if you are the same "blood type," and there still may be some difficulty in your body accepting blood from other people.

In the healthcare industry, they are called "blood groups" and not "blood types." The Blancos are fully aware that the "sugars" you know as A, B, and Rh cause the most severe immune response, and A, B, and Rh are sugars that rise off the surface of the red blood cell. Type O just means that you do not have these types of sugars on your blood surface, but it does not mean that you have none whatsoever.

There are millions of blood groups, but the A and B types along with Rh cause the greatest reaction, so these are the "antigens" or sugars that the Blancos look for to encourage a successful outcome when blood is needed by a patient. To represent the Rh factor, they simply place a plus (+) or a minus (–) sign by the A, B, O, and AB types to inform them of how to match up donor to recipient.

So just know that if you are the same "blood type" as someone, things should potentially work out in your favor, and the rule of thumb for them is that AB+ is a universal recipient and O- is a universal donor, The reason for this is because AB+ blood type has all of the "antigens" or sugars and can theoretically accept blood from all the blood types, and O- has none of the most reactive antigens and should be able to give blood to each group. Just commit to memory that this does not mean that this is your blood type as much as it is the antigens that they look for which could cause an adverse immune response.

Now you see how important sugar or Karbon is to the blood, but because they have become shrewd by naming it many different things, and because they have convinced you that it's nothing more than "red liquid," you are quick to give it away and, even more important, you overlook that it is desired by the organism you know as yeast, or the sugar fungus!

Imagine a whole food supply geared around feeding this beast inside you! Why do you think the Blancos have stated that their best invention was "sliced bread"?! If this organism is not of any importance, why do you think in certain religions the bread represents the body of Christ, or unleavened bread is used in religious rites? Have I not proved to you before that "science" merely picks up where religion left off!

You must always be aware that this is the reason as melanin beings that our science and religion was one, and that the dichotomy created by the Blancos was a way to cause confusion and a way to create mystery in the mind of the chosen class. We must always remember that the Most High is not the author of confusion! This organism shares our entire body with us!

"Our skin surface, ears, noses, mouths, vaginas, and digestive systems teem with a variety of yeasts" (Money, 2018, 16).

The book, titled *The Rise of Yeast,* goes on further to state,

"Dandruff is related to the growth of a yeast called *Malassezia globosa* in skin flakes, and it is controlled by antifungal agents incorporated into medical shampoos. *Malassezia* consumes fatty sebum secreted into hair follicles and competes for food with resident *Demodex* mites. Swarming with yeast and mites, we are walking ecosystems" (Money, 2018, 16).

So, they know damn well what the root cause of hair loss is, when you have a fungus that eats the *sebum* or the oil that is responsible for nourishing the hair, how can the hair grow? Instead, what do these wicked and evil beings do? They just create something to control it, making sure you are able to live with the condition, and never think twice about how to get rid of it! Because you have lived this way for most of your life, when the process of repair is started, you must be patient enough to give yourself years to recuperate.

Once again, I have to remind you that this Khemistry is not unfamiliar to the people who knew the power of manipulating this organism. What is easy to notice when you look at the cover of the book, *The Rise of Yeast,* is that the yeast is in the shape of the pyramids, because we all know and should always commit to memory that the world is ruled by signs and symbols. For those who need more confirmation, the author states, "105,000-year-old stone tools in Africa provide some clues about the first drinks brewed by our species" (Money, 2018, 28).

The author goes on further and states,

"'Ombike,' which is a traditional home-brewed liquor of the Aawambo people in Namibia and Angola. Starch grains from wild sorghum seeds were also found on stone tools. Sorghum beer has been brewed for millennia and remains very popular in southern Africa" (Money, 2018, 28).

So, manipulating this organism was nothing new to our people, and, as always, it was done in a way that encouraged balance in Nature and within the community. In the twentieth century, a debate raged within the "scientific community" and that was the role that saturated fats played in the role of heart disease. This campaign was touted as one free of the influence of multinational corporations and articulated as a concern by the establishment for the welfare and well-being of the public.

According to the establishment, a diet consisting of monounsaturated and polyunsaturated fats could help lower cholesterol and combat heart disease. The amazing thing about all this is, is that the Blancos call these "edible oils" vegetable oils, when they come from seeds! The oil from the seeds is mechanically extracted then *purified* as well as refined or Khemically altered. Why would something lauded as being beneficial for heart health have to be refined and purified before it can be consumed, especially if its source is from "vegetables"?

Take canola oil, for instance. Because of its high erucic acid content, it was banned in some countries. The plant's original name was the rapeseed plant. The erucic acid levels actually caused heart attacks instead of preventing them, so the "food product" was initially banned by some governments.

Then, of course, after lowering the acid levels and renaming rapeseed oil to canola oil, which is actually an acronym for "Canada oil low acid," the Canadian government then decided it was ok to sell to the public. Now we know the danger is hidden right there in the name!

Then, as the kindhearted and concerned parents that the government claims to be, they slapped a GRAS (Generally Recognized As Safe) label on that sucka and started mass production of a "food product," which was initially known to cause heart attacks. Brothers and sisters, would it surprise you to know this was just the side show?!

"Six vegetable oils were examined for their yeast and mould contaminants. Sixteen yeasts and 35 mould species were isolated from the oil samples. The isolates were members of the following genera: *Saccharomyces, Candida, Debaromyces, Hansenula, Trichosporon, Torulopsis* and *Pichia* for yeasts and *Aspergillus, Fusarium, Penicillium, Mucor, Geotrichum* and *Cladosporium* for moulds. Among the two groups of fungi, *Saccharomyces* and *Aspergillus* species predominated" (Okpokwasili & Molokwu, 1996).

This is the reason the Blancos desire for you to cook and prepare most of your staple foods with these oils, because they are loaded with fungus and molds, which wreak havoc on the body causing myriad illnesses that they claim are "etiology unknown!" The experiments conducted by these scientists were for the purposes of seeing how resilient these oils were to biodeterioration, which was caused by these organisms, upon which coconut oil had the lowest rate and palm oil had the highest rate.

We melanin beings are not surprised that coconut oil was more resilient, because we are aware that it contains antifungal properties that do not encourage growth of these organisms. It is also worth noting that the most powerful antifungal medications are synthetic versions of coconut oil! I have told you once, and I shall say it again with force and conviction, you are giving someone credit for going in their lab and *reverse-engineering nature*! When will you wake up and realize that artificial intelligence, or AI will never eclipse natural technology?!

If there is one thing you must commit to memory about this organism, it is that yeast is a perfect weapon against the human being. The reason for this is because it is a eukaryotic cell, or basically a cell with a nucleus, and we as humans are in this category as well. This is the main reason why this organism is of great importance to the "scientific community" when concocting bioweapons against humanity, specifically because of this key similarity.

This fungus also secretes alcohol as it feeds off sugar, and it just so happens, this is how it eliminates other species of fungus that compete within the same environment. All fungus has a tipping point, where they can only tolerate so much alcohol in the environment and *Saccharomyces* just so happens to be at the top of the food chain in this regard. This is the reason why in the above experiments conducted by the "scientists," they noted that *Saccharomyces* happened to be one of the species in the majority because other species could not tolerate alcohol at the levels that *Saccharomyces* can. As they argue that fungus allows for a greater understanding of the human organism, it is misleading to assume that what is learned remains within the confines of lab experiments and scientific journals.

You must know everything they learn they *apply* to the human population without the care for its drawbacks and ramifications.

> "Genetically modified (GM) yeast strains are used to produce a range of drugs including human insulin, vaccines, and an injectable medicine to treat eye degeneration . . . The vaccine against the human papillomavirus (HPV), which is the dominant cause of cervical cancer . . . In nature they contribute to the decomposition part of the carbon cycle by digesting substances produced by plants and animals or dissolving the post-mortem remains of their tissues" (Money, 2018, 15).

Did I not tell you that this organism will consume you from the inside out? I have told you that the main objective of this organism is to consume the entire vessel of the melanin being, if left unchecked or ignored! Look at the "food products" in the Blanco supermarkets. They give you leavened bread where this organism sits and incubates, gaining strength because of the high fructose corn syrup laden in the "food product." They create this raging bull, if you will, because *Saccharomyces* cerevisiae ferments glucose faster than it does fructose, so by the time it invades your system, it is ready to destroy everything in its path in an effort to establish its dominance.

This organism is fueled by oxygen as well, so what better host to invade than a host that literally has to breathe oxygen to survive! Imagine an organism that prefers to feed on the fuel that is the *only* sugar or only form of Karbon that the blood chooses to run on! As I have said before, there is literally a vampire feeding inside of you!

Forgive me if it feels that I have to revisit these sources too many times, but unfortunately the weight of my conviction and position in many cases has never been enough to jar the melanin mind from its deep slumber. Unfortunately, too many of our warriors and whistleblowers have faced the same manner of disbelief and cynicism. How many of us or our children have allergies, specifically the ones dealing with the outside world? And we tend to think it is just our disconnect with Nature and that pollen levels are too high, making Nature's world unbearable. This fungus can shed spores on stalks and then release them as dust in the wind,

"The combination of these passive and active mechanisms distributes millions of tons of spores into the air every year, affecting the chemistry of the atmosphere and causing hundreds of millions of asthmatics to wheeze" (Money, 2018, 35).

Recall that this monster is in his lab with the intentions to curb the population growth and claims that "viruses" will be the cause of this apocalyptic eventuality, yet, interestingly enough, fungus has the exact same attributes of "viruses" and is the only mechanism that can officially go airborne and cause the desired outcome by the elite. They claim "viruses" but yet spend all their time researching and genetically modifying fungus!

Recall that the first "viruses" isolated were from those that came from plants! Even though they know that plants are always under constant attack from fungus, their "scientists" concluded that it must be something else, because as you know, they are Blancos, and they say so. If you have not noticed by now, the Blancos do not have to be right, they just have to agree with one another, specifically those apart of the "scientific community."

Think about this critically, brothers and sisters, if "viruses" can have a long incubation period, waxing and waning in virulence potential, then why not use a fungus that can multiply into biblical proportions, a few cells evolving into *billions overnight*!? Just look at the human immunodeficiency virus (HIV) that causes AIDS. When it first came out, people were dropping like flies, then they convinced us that even *without* being diagnosed, you could be living with it for years.

Remember, as their "science" states, a "virus" needs access to your DNA to replicate itself, a fungus does not! The key to the idea of "retro viruses" was the discovery of a concept called "reverse transcriptase." This meant in lay terms that because DNA was primarily in the nucleus, "science" had to get around the "central dogma," which was that "once 'information' has passed into the protein it cannot get out again" (Klug, 2004).

Well, how Blanco "scientists" got around this Swiss

cheese explanation of bio-Khemistry was to suggest that the "viruses" used RNA to make DNA! See, RNA is in the cytoplasm of the cell and, as stated earlier, DNA is in the nucleus, so in order to get around the "central dogma" of their own pseudoscience, they found a way to make this "virus" idea work. So now, the linear transfer of information does not apply, where DNA makes RNA, which makes more DNA. Now it can go in reverse! Now RNA can make DNA, which would now allow "viruses" to copy themselves and take over the host, hence the term "reverse transcriptase!"

This thinking was indispensable to bringing a factual basis to the idea of retroviruses, such as HIV, and nonretroviral "viruses," such as hepatitis B. Reverse transcriptase was discovered by Howard Temin but isolated by David Baltimore in 1970. Talk about coincidence, literally a decade before the AIDS outbreak, which also Dr. *Fraudci* was heavily invested in!

There was an article published by the *Washington Post* on May 9, 1989, written by Larry Thompson, titled, "Science under Fire behind the Clash between Congress and Nobel Laureate David Baltimore." In the first paragraph it plainly states,

"Congress, which funds nearly half of all biomedical research in this country, is questioning whether the scientific community can continue to police itself, or whether stricter regulations are needed" (Thompson, 1989).

US House of Representative John Dingell from Michigan was sure something was afoul as it seemed the scientific process was being subverted in order to initiate an agenda. A senior Dingell staffer who was in charge of the Baltimore investigation was reported as saying, "It's hard to tell if it's error or fraud. At certain times, it appears to be fraud and other times, misrepresentation" (Thompson, 1989). It's funny the language they use when confronting those in power who abuse power! If I were to "misrepresent" myself to police officers, I don't think they would have any trouble at all charging me with a crime! But I digress. The article goes on further to state,

"On the average, a good scientific paper is cited about once a year over a 15-year period ... According to a special ISI [Institute for Scientific Information] review, the disputed Cell [journal] paper has been cited 30 times in three years—10 times more than average" (Thompson, 1989).

Is it just by chance that David Baltimore also became one of the leading spokespersons for HIV/AIDS, securing tons of money from the government in order to combat the "disease"? When asked by the committee how he stumbled on such a huge discovery, David Baltimore called it "a bit of luck" (Thompson, 1989). The article goes on to detail how about 30 percent of "scientific" reports that are published are *never* heard from again! In closing, the article states,

"How much fraud exists in science—which is mostly funded through taxpayers dollars—is not clear. Many scientists argue there is little; Dingell committee staffers believe it is much more common and that the scientific community is not capable of policing itself" (Thompson, 1989).

If the "science" is so sound, one would argue why is there any fraud to begin with? Even the "scientists" agreed that there was some but suggested that there is "little." Once again, I will ask you where were the Black leaders? You must know that I am not talking about the ones in Congress, we know they are already bought and paid for. I am talking about the ones who profess to be diehard revolutionaries! If I found this information, then how in the hell did they not find it? Even so-called revolutionaries today do not dig as deep and continue to spew out the same talking points and inflammatory rhetoric to get you charged, talking about how they pushed AIDS in the ghettos and yet Congress was at a point in time trying to figure out whether it even existed!

I told you I am here to wake you up; other Negroes are here to make the bed! Because of these high-level manipulation tactics, you ignore what has always been a force for and against human beings since the dawn of civilization, and the ignorance of this organism will lead our people to their demise. Now you have come one step closer to understanding why alcohol was illegal in the early part of the twentieth century, not because it was an issue taken up by religious organizations, or the government putting forth an effort to curb the degradation of society, because if this was the case, both organizational bodies would have made sure that they outlawed *every* illicit drug, not just alcohol.

The concept, in our era, that alcohol is legal and most other illicit drugs have been deemed illegal proves that they knew the power of the yeast organism and could not allow it to be unleashed on their own population until they could genetically engineer the organism to benefit the Blancos. Notice that the ignorance of Khemistry widens and deepens the divide between reality and the Godbody. Now that we know how aggressive this organism is in its nature, let's just look at a couple of terms to relieve the melanin mind of all doubt of its destructive abilities.

Candidiasis is a fungal infection that is usually an overgrowth of fungus on the skin or mucous membranes caused by the yeast candida. The most invasive and the most common form of this fungal overgrowth is called candidemia. This overgrowth invades the bloodstream, colonizing virtually every organ in the body, resulting in long hospital stays and death, the latter becoming more prevalent because the "doctors" have to test for it before they can take any action against it, and because most "doctors" are disgusted with patients who come in and relate every ailment to a fungal overgrowth, they tend to chalk it up as "heart disease," "stroke," or a fast-spreading "cancer" with no known cure.

What the Blancos hate is the idea of a multibillion-dollar industry built on myriad "diseases" being reduced to one species as the explanation, Besides surgery, what would be the point of going to visit a moron in a lab coat, just for them to tell you that "we need to run more tests"? Is it not interesting that the very fluid that the fungus feeds on is the very fluid they have to test to get an accurate reading of why the body cannot return back to homeostasis?

These people just position themselves as individuals who have authority over life and death! They are no different than a judge or a police officer, given the title of judge, jury, and executioner and nothing more. We fail to realize that if these people knew what was really going on, they would be leading the best lives themselves. Instead, in order to gain access to effective treatment, a person must go to a "specialist" or a "holistic practitioner," which in most cases is not covered by the patient's insurance company.

Is it not odd that the true science, the science of Khemistry, is not recognized by the corporate bloodsuckers known as insurance companies? Those companies were not created to *assure* you, they were created to *ensure* that you will have no clue of what is going on. Out of all the mysteries of life, they desire for your vessel to be the greatest mystery of all, because once one knows themself, all the mysteries of the cosmos will be made known to them.

Now that you have an idea of how dark, corrupt, and vile these beings are, does it not make your blood boil to look at the commercials and ads for these corporations as they claim to be "family oriented," "building better futures," and any other highly deceptive marketing schemes that allow them to create the vampire inside of you?

You must already know from what has been discussed, that yeast's waste product is alcohol. Some people get so much of this waste in their bloodstream, that if they were to take a breathalyzer test, they would fail, and this is without having one drink at all! The condition is called auto-brewery syndrome!

As has been stated before, once they began to understand the importance of the organism and its ability to become many things, they would then build a system centered around this aspect of our Khemistry. As you know by now, I was born in the state of Michigan, and the city of Battle Creek is known as Cereal City, the home of Kellogg and Post cereal companies.

The story goes that the Kellogg brothers created their cereal for people who were suffering from an imbalance created by an overgrowth of yeast, imbalances such as dyspepsia, indigestion, and the "great American stomach-ache." They would treat these people, often famous people who were top men in industry and even a president or two.

In the late 1800s, "Doctor" Kellogg felt that the digestive process could be hastened if the grains were precooked and "predigested." The heat would break down the starch content, which we have identified as a sugar in the category of polysaccharides, into the simple sugar called dextrose. One of the problems, among many, when it comes to processed cereals is that the bran and the germ from the grain has been removed, and it is easily broken down in the mouth, which we have already confirmed is one of the incubators of the sugar fungus. It's also the main reason as to why so many people have outbreaks around the mouth when they entertain a diet such as this.

When John Harvey Kellogg went on a trip, his brother Will came up with the idea to add sugar to cornflakes and, lo and behold, Frosted Flakes cereal was born. If you grew up in the 1980s, during the explosion of processed cereals, then you may have eaten a bowl or two of Frosted Flakes. And you know full well that it didn't need to break down in the mouth, because by the time you got to your fourth spoonful, the flakes had already broken down in the milk, too soggy to be of any good, although I'm sure some would disagree. What's also interesting to note is that the Kellogg brothers were Seventh-day Adventists, which further reinforces the idea that "science" had merely picked up where religion had left off.

The point here is that, like all the foods we consume, fungus plays a huge role in its evolution. The problem is that once the Blancos had figured this out, they began to saturate our markets with foodstuffs that were the basic building blocks for exponential growth of yeast inside the human body. Just as your shampoos and lotions have chemicals in them to slow down the growth of the yeast, the same can be said of the food you consume so that it increases "shelf life." The closer a food is to Nature, the faster it can be broken down by the sugar fungus.

Life is about balance, so the body can use these organisms to help facilitate the myriad complex Khemical reactions that take place twenty-four hours a day, but as with anything, too much can be downright deadly.

If you remember from what was mentioned earlier, supposedly the Kellogg brothers did this to serve the public and to solve the health issues of the times and bring humans one step closer to harmony within the self, so harmony could be achieved outside the self. If this was true, considering that cereal is now considered to be at the top of the breakfast world, why are so many of our people diabetic as well as suffering from illnesses, such as atherosclerosis, high cholesterol, and high blood pressure?

Also, if it has nothing to do with us receiving the brunt end of all this fraudulent "science," then how come we represent a fraction of the population and yet lead in these areas of poor health? If you ask me, it sounds eerily similar to the social disease of mass incarceration. You have to realize this is an all-out war against your people! How in the hell can a people who are now a minority in their own country be at the top of the list in all of the wrong categories in every area of life activity? They are so hellbent on our destruction, that any Blancos they lose in the process in order to complete the objective is seen as a necessary evil.

As I have said, they will turn many from one. When your toddler has an overgrowth of yeast in the mouth, they do not come out and say it in a way so that you are reminded of the power of this fungus. What they do is call it by a name that seems benign in Nature, like "oral thrush." They are aware of the depths the machine has gone to in order to cover up the truth, but because we have been cursed with the other vampire living inside of us, that most of us refer to as the god complex of the Blancos, we will not question the information given to us.

Also, what does it matter if you dig during your research, but you only go deep enough to uncover the top-soil, when you know full well the answers are casket deep. It's an old adage that is very popular within the Black community that states, "if you want to hide something from a Black person, then put it in a book." We know, as revolutionaries, this is untrue because true revolution-aries know that reading is only half the battle, because "if you cannot understand what you have read, then you, sir, cannot read."

Would it even matter if the government decided to break up big business with antitrust laws, when everyone thinks the same? The American people along with the melanin beings are not debating that the nature of busi-ness should stop. They're only debating why its piece of the pie should be a little bigger.

In 2019, a movie based on real events was released, and the title of that film was *Dark Waters*. The film was about an attorney, played by actor Mark Ruffalo, who stands up to a "chemical giant" by the name of the DuPont company that was poisoning a local town's water supply. The reason why the process was moving so slowly in terms of getting justice for the people affected in West Virginia was not just because DuPont was a "chemical giant," but it was an economic staple of West Virginia, supplying good paying jobs to thousands of people in the area.

The local government was slow to take action because we all know what happens to cities and towns when big business decides to up and leave and outsource its services to areas that would allow them to cut costs of production. Its "chemicals" that are used for coating tanks would be the same "chemicals" used to make "nonstick pans." The "chemical" runoff would make its way into the ecosystem, killing livestock and obviously human beings. For a while, the "chemicals" were just added to the drinking water, just to see the effects that it would have on the local population, but all this would be ignored. Not just because Americans would choose a life of luxury and convenience over quality of life, it had more to do with the ignorance of Khemistry.

When the lawyer had the "Khemistry" explained to him by a "chemist," and the adverse reactions that had come about due to these long chains of Karbon and hydrogen, it shook him to his core! He began tearing up the flooring and the carpets, even throwing away the pots and pans, much to the dismay of his wife, who was clueless about the environment around her, after realizing that they literally had "chemical deathtraps" around themselves and their child, that corporate America had convinced them would make their house into a home.

He finally sat her down to explain to her what was going on because he appeared to be a madman, acting out without any rhyme or reason until the Khemistry was explained and made known to her. What he realized, was even though he was a successful lawyer, that meant absolutely *nothing* to the world of Khemistry, the real wizard in this land of Oz.

This is why the "science" is so heinous. If there ever was a day that melanin beings were able to get reparations, we know for sure that the money would go right back into the coffers in the devil's shipyard. As you can see from all the evidence right in front of you, and from the Blancos' own mouths as they have characterized this as the sixth wave of extinction, there is no way that we as melanin beings can use their "science" to restore Mother Earth back to her original glory and splendor, nor the people who are a spitting image of such brilliance. We have allowed the Blancos to make a mockery of us while they piggyback on Mother Nature's genius and then proclaim, "Anything you can do, I can do better."

They created Gatorade and claimed that it "hydrates better than water" (Schaefer, 2018), but yet has water in it! If you are so much greater than Mother Nature, create your own version of water, and then place it in your concoctions and see how far you get. Hydro, according to their "scientists," means *water*, so how can something do a job better than water when we know, as previously mentioned, that water is critical to the fourth state of matter?

And there is nothing on earth made by humans that can change that! The machine has evolved into an industry which has maintained an iron grip on the perception of what is true health.

"A snippet from a new PBS *Frontline* report called 'Fat,' which featured the chair of Harvard's Department of Nutrition, Walter Willet, pointing the finger directly at the food companies. 'The transition of food to being an industrial product really has been a fundamental problem,' Willet said. 'First, the actual processing has stripped away the nutritional value of the food. Most of the grains have been converted to starches. We have sugar in concentrated form, and many of the fats have been concentrated and then, worst of all, hydrogenated, which creates trans-fatty acids with very adverse effects on health'" (Moss, 2013, xvii).

They are deliberately contaminating foods in order to destabilize the health and well-being of the masses, and because our ignorance of the true science is a key part of the socializing process, it can only be perceived as an act of war on the part of the establishment. Is this to say that Blancos do not have a fight on their hands, as well as the establishment, as they sink their tentacles into the foundation of the human soul? Certainly, this does not, but unfortunately the source from where our energies arise come from two different origins.

The problem is that the drive for control, from these people, has outweighed the concern for balance. In order to restore this balance, the vanguards of this realm need to be restored to their rightful places designated by the cosmos. I have always said that the most insidious flaw of their "science" is this notion that you can treat disease with disease.

- They used cowpox to treat smallpox.
- They use genetically modified yeast to treat an overgrowth of yeast.
- They use attenuated or weakened forms of a "virus" to fight a "virus."

It's almost as if they have the mentality of two brutes in the boxing ring, and may the most destructive force win, claiming it a victory, even if the host does not survive the conflict. This is the same approach they use when creating and manufacturing the highly processed foods that have become a staple of the American diet.

"Salt, sugar, and fat are an entirely different game. Not only are they not accidental contaminants like E. *coli*, the industry methodically studies and controls their use" (Moss, 2013, xxv).

So, when we hear about Escherichia coli (E. coli) and salmonella outbreaks, we think that it was just a mistake that has occurred, or a lapse of judgment on the part of an employee or an executive. But in reality it is the deliberate use of these organisms that play a crucial role in product viability and, even more sinister, the engineering of the human genome. We have not been ready to realize the lengths this system will go to in order to obtain complete control over a realm that grants melanin beings access to the greatest experience.

The knowledge of how this industry works as it is fueled by the hidden science of alkhemy, or Khemistry if you will, is of the utmost importance to the health and well-being of the melanin being. As we move into expounding on the second head of this two-headed monster, we have to realize that the reverse-engineering of Nature is key to the illusion, along with outright theft of our accomplishments, which contributes heavily to the perception we call the god complex plaguing the mind of the melanin being.

It is one of the most perplexing issues of our time. How will we as melanin beings unite, if there is so much hatred and indifference being shown to one another? The first step in this fight is to control our image! On how many occasions has reality contradicted or been in sharp contrast to the statistics being spewed by so-called experts? We cannot underestimate how critically important it is to control how we see ourselves, because it will determine how we treat one another! If this is not rectified, we will continue to treat one another as slaves who are fighting for an opportunity to become the "house Negro," while simultaneously keeping the Blancos in the mindset that speaks to a god nature.

If our image is not important, tell me with a straight face, that shows like *Maury* and *Jerry Springer* did not cause irreparable damage to the image of the Black man and the Black woman! We failed to realize that these images were not just produced for entertainment in the United States, but these images were produced for the *whole world to see*! These images give the impression that the melanin being is irresponsible, immature, and in need of the paternalistic relationship that exists between the Blancos and the chosen class.

This is the reason why I place so much emphasis on promoting the strengths of our brothers and sisters, encouraging those who have platforms to center themselves around repair and revolution, rather than fruitless debates and topics that center around justification for the divide and the grim reality of its outcomes. The image of a people is so powerful that it can swallow up the progress and contributions of the individual, yet the individual can be isolated and used to mold the image of the people, because the power of the media is used to define the character of a nation.

So, for instance, no matter how much I accomplish on a local level, whether it's starting and running my own business, raising my children to become responsible adults, or treating my Black queen with the respect and honor that she deserves, it means nothing to the meager minds that have bought into the propaganda. On the other hand, if I were to commit crimes and produce children out of wedlock, all it takes is for one of these stigmas to make the news and it reinforces the strength of the grip it has on the reputation of our people.

This is why we use plural terms when we see the mistakes of one individual. We may see a Black man or a Black woman who has found themselves on the other side of the law, and we immediately say, "Black people" need to get their stuff together. Or we may say "*we*" just can't get right. Although when there is a great accomplishment by one of our people, it does not bleed into the image of the collective, it only remains within the confines of the individual's efforts that are being highlighted. We say "good for him," or "good for her," the opposite reaction when something negative happens that affects our image and our community.

This is the sole reason that I only choose to focus on the strengths of my community and its members, because I am already aware of all the negative press our melanin warriors receive. So, in all there must be a source of inspiration that my people can draw from to combat the overwhelming flow of negative energy that steers public perception, which in turn has a direct effect on the outcome of public policy.

A perfect example was already given using Willie Horton and George Bush Sr. as an example. As you can see, our image needs to be safeguarded, because it can prevent us from achieving upward mobility in society, determine the nature of police interactions, influence the likelihood of procuring long-lasting relationships (intimate or platonic), and even elevating politicians to the highest seat in the land! This is how important your image is!

Even more important, while you are stuck raising yourself from the mud, Blancos are spending their time creating 5G networks, planning trips to Mars, and polishing the nose on their nuclear warheads. So, when you have been reduced to wallowing in the mud, the only recourse is to hop on social media on the Blancos TV shows and social platforms and air out your dirty laundry. This is not just a gap between the rich and the poor; this is an ever-widening gap between ignorance and social currency.

As W.E.B. DuBois pointed out, social currency is the trade of ideas between a group of people, which aids in accelerating their development, which inevitably secures a place in time for future generations (Green & Smith, 1993). This chasm that is visible between species is the foundation on which the god complex rests on, positioned comfortably and undisturbed from even seismic shifts in the consciousness of the melanin beings, due to the ignorance or denial of their rightful position.

We also fail to realize this is a global effort on the part of the system to convince us that our purpose in this realm is to be nothing more than servants and entertainers for the rest of humankind, given free reign of creative expression so long as we romanticize lifestyles that place poverty, Black death, incarceration, and misogyny on a pedestal.

Nowadays, in social media, there is a group of men within our community who profess that the way to battle the emasculation of the Black male is to replace it with the unwavering position of the alpha male. I am in no means in opposition to the strong Black male image, but I am also aware of the dangers in becoming a fundamentalist in any area of life activity. If we attack this idea with brutal honesty, we must admit that the bar that this society has set for manhood has been the bar set by Blanco men.

Even though we can argue about what has been taken from us that was integral to building their industries, we know, according to their logic, that possession is nine-tenths of the law, and they are the ones who make the laws. Because they have positioned themselves as the leaders of the "free world," the Black man is in last place, at best, in this Western thought process of leadership and global dominance. So, seeing as how at this moment in time, we cannot outman the man, if you will, why is it that our treatment of our women differ dramatically in representation? If we choose to cater to our women, this type of man is seen as soft and weak, perplexing the outsider as to how one can hold up a family unit when they show no traces of a backbone.

As stated before, everything is about balance. No one should be taken advantage of regardless of gender, so the man should definitely not be a pushover. But once again, because we have accepted this role of second- or third-class alpha male to the Blancos, then it is only right that we contrast their behavior as it relates to their women, versus the behavior we showcase to ours.

There is a genre of movies called "romance movies," as well as a ton of "romantic novels," etc., and as one can already point out, this term suggests this is the way they have treated their women since the days of their antiquity, even though we know otherwise, but the obvious need not be stated. The word "Rome in this term should be the dead giveaway. So even when our women say that they want "Rome-mance," they are stating without even realizing it that they prefer if you would treat them like the Blanco man treats his woman. And if you think this is a stretch, then just ask anyone about the "image" of Italy where Rome is and try to deny its image of romance.

The point is, we as melanin beings know how much of a warmonger the Blancos can be, that does not stop them from making movies and writing novels about how they would go to the ends of the earth to be with the man or the woman they love. On the other hand, the way we treat our women, as conveyed through the media, has its roots in films about pimps and playas, so even if we do find the woman who we want to spend the rest of our life with, it's usually after we get caught up sleeping with any woman we can get our hands on.

The point here is that the Blanco man is able to keep his alpha male status, no matter how much "simpin" he may do in his movies and in his books he sells to her. The main reason for this, is that at the end of the day, he controls his own image, and that image can be summed up as the leader of the "free world." You must realize as well, that this position will always be secure, because it is a byproduct of the god complex.

Think about it, his military is everywhere, the god he gave you to serve is everywhere, hell, even the Santa Claus he made up knows whether or not your children are being naughty or nice. He makes movies about traveling to outer space and finding portals that teleports him to other dimensions, and yet the melanin mind is fooled into believing this type of propaganda has no effect on the psyche. Even the money you work so hard to get, so you can provide for you and your family has his face on it! Think about why putting Harriet Tubman on the twenty-dollar bill caused so much controversy, because the Blancos understand the power of *image*!

To drive this point home, if you recall the 1988 movie, *Coming to America* (the classic, not the 2021 *Coming 2 America*), the most powerful part of that movie, which a lot of people overlooked, was when Mr. McDowell realized how powerful Prince Akeem was when he received the money with his face on it. He said something to the effect of, "the boy has got his own money" (Landis, 1988).

Countries showcase their power by issuing their own currency, and politically speaking, the way you weaken a country is through the devaluation of its dollar! As always, commit to memory that the world is ruled by signs and symbols. As stated earlier, this is a global effort to remake the earth into their liking and to their choosing, and, unfortunately, people of color are nowhere in that equation.

In Brazil there is a competition called Globeleza. In 2014, a Brazilian dancer by the name of Nayara Justino had her crown taken away from her because of her dark skin tone. Ironically enough, this pageant is centered around African heritage, but Brazilians are used to lighter skin representing the pageant, and essentially all of Brazil for that matter. She received backlash from the entire country for literally being the quintessence of what the pageant was all about. Brazil could care less, because we all know that the closer you are to the skin tone reflective of world rulership, the closer you are to gaining respect and a nominal sense of autonomy among the Western power bloc on the geopolitical stage.

Because we think that colorism is unique to the United States, we surmise that what we are attracted to is a result of our own making, but in reality, what you are attracted to are the *images* that you have been fed since you were a child! This is the importance of *imagery*! Adults oftentimes forget there are always new minds born into the world who can take on a different outlook or worldview, depending on what images they find themselves at the mercy of. The powers that be know this as well, and they know if they use their mediums of information exchange to promote a lifestyle, skin tone, a mode of behavior, etc., you will inevitably see cases of life imitating art.

When we look at countries like India and the Caribbean Islands and, unfortunately, the Motherland, this self-hate has morphed into an all-out war on melanin as many of our women and men as well, use skin-lightening creams in order to achieve the false standard of beauty. Worldwide, in 2020, women of color spent $8.6 billion on skin-lightening creams to become a part of this deadly vanity. "The market is projected to reach $12.3 billion by 2027" (*The Conversation,* 2021). Because, as we all know, losing the power of melanin increases the chances of acquiring skin cancer.

Conveniently enough, this is also the group that is used to argue that Black people get skin cancer too, but yet they fail to disclose the reason as to why this is so. Can you imagine vanity causing you to turn your back on the Most High's highest representation of her power, the central power source of radiation we call the Sun, all to satisfy an empty desire to be accepted by a people who will destroy their own!

How many times have you heard the argument from someone who will say that Blancos have no mercy on their own, so it's not just a "White and Black thing." Is this supposed to comfort me and dull my senses until it nullifies the hatred I have for the system? *Of course not!* The most important reason why this is so, is because I know that this is not a part of my people's nature! We know that we had advanced civilizations and were adept at Khemistry, so if this is the case, why did we not invent guns and stockpile nuclear weapons to fight against each other?

We have already determined that Africa is a continent that can house almost all the other "continents" inside of its landmass, yet there was only one country in Africa that ever had nuclear weapons, and that was the country controlled by Blancos that they named South Africa. Those weapons were later dismantled, so up to this day, there is no country in Africa that has nuclear weapons, yet it is the largest landmass on this so-called planet.

The Black man is propagated around the world as a villain and a criminal, yet the United States can drop hydrogen bombs on foreign land and level cities, destroying not just humans but also ecosystems, and still be seen as humanitarian and a lover of animals and plant life!

The Black man and the Black woman are propagated as drug dealers and drug addicts, yet Big Pharma can shake the US to its core, achieving the milestone of six times more people addicted to prescription medication than all "illegal" drugs *combined.*

This species can murder its own at a level that can annihilate everything in its path, and that is what makes us different from our counterparts. But because they control their own *image*, they will always be able to leave the battles of public opinion unscathed.

Have you ever noticed that melanin beings can be held accountable for their actions, but the Blancos have to wait until Judgment Day? Your mother or father will tell you, "Be careful out there in that world because if you do wrong, you will end up in somebody's jail or in somebody's casket and that will be the end of it." But when you ask them when will the Blancos receive judgment, they say, "We have to wait on God to come back to take care of them."

We have made ourselves so small and insignificant that we hope, plead, and beg that God will come back to do the work, because, of course, your little frail and childlike minds don't have the intelligence to defeat your boogeymen. You find though that when the Blancos have a problem on this planet, they do not marinate in a puddle of their own despair and weakness, they shout out a war cry that says, "Praise the Lord, and pass the ammunition!"

All throughout their history, they have been telling you that the greatest asset they have as human beings is their willingness to die for what they believe in. They even have another saying by US President Thomas Jefferson; "The tree of liberty must be refreshed from time to time with the blood of patriots and tyrants" (Jefferson, 1787).

As it was noted, this god complex is at work in *every area of life activity*! I find that when melanin beings say that they don't believe in a Blanco god, they are ruled by his money; if they are not ruled by his money, then they are ruled by his women; if they are not ruled by his women, then they are ruled by his "science." So, if every area of life activity does not go through a cleansing process, then the Blancos will continue to exert a power over you that will reinforce the god complex.

I've even heard of Negroes who pacify the people with talks of building schools, as if they decide when and where the wars will be. These second- and third-tier alpha males are forced back into the beta position as soon as the Blancos decide to shut down his country.

- How many "hood niggas" have a gangster reputation in the community and will easily get rid of one of their own, but as soon as the cops come, they lose that crazy behavior and become sane and put their hands over their heads and are taken into custody without incident?
- How many of our churchgoers in the Black community will pat themselves on the back about how they live a drug-free life, but as soon as the Blancos prescribe medication that has been fast-tracked and possibly life-threatening, they take it without question?
- How many Blacks say they would never be a "slave," like the ones in the narrative that is told by Blanco history and yet when a sentence is handed down, they find themselves crying behind bars?
- How many "revolutionaries" scream Black Power and economic empowerment for the underclass, yet as soon as they take the people's money, they tell you to get it how you live?

The liberation that is desired is one that should free you in *every area of life activity*: economics, education, entertainment, labor, law, politics, sex, religion, and war. Until then, we are a group of slaves masquerading around as if we were emancipated, parroting useless stratagems and methods that at the very least are outdated, and at most exercises in futility.

When my son was born in 2018, there was a spark that was lit inside of me, a drive that required no fuel to keep the engine running. I knew I had a herculean task in front of me, but because I felt myself living for someone else, I became an unstoppable force ready to confront the immovable object. The Most High had at that moment transformed my future to an open book, and without reading a word I knew exactly what the first chapter was about.

In order to secure his future, I may have to sacrifice mine in the process. Preparing yourself to die does not mean that you will, it just means that you are prepared to do so if you have to. My son made me realize something beautiful about Mother Nature, that every new creation was a new possibility, a new and unique expression of cosmic energy with the old responsibility of upholding and defending truth.

I cannot say that this was just a moment of elation and joy, it can be more accurately described as being fixed in a state of ambivalence. On one hand, I was proud to be a father and caretaker of a golden child, but on the other hand, I knew that he had been born among a sea of wolves, ready to devour him the moment one mistake is made.

"In 2005, records obtained by Public Employees for Environmental Responsibility showed a sharp increase in the number of cooperative research and development agreements with companies and trade associations under the administration. The group's report noted that the American Chemistry Council had become the EPA's 'leading research partner.'

One of the joint projects with the chemistry council was a study . . . for continuing to spray pesticides in rooms used by their babies and infants, to observe their health effects. The study was canceled following expressions of public outrage at the prospect of using kids as test animals" (Shabecoff & Shabecoff, 2010, 156).

But this is exactly how they see our children and our brothers and sisters who are not just connected by god-molecule melanin, but also in mind and spirit. As you have just learned in the above statement, this "chemistry council" has us under constant attack, threatening the future of our young ones, by compromising the balance of Mother Earth. When we think about Khemistry, we never realize how huge this hidden science is! It is so huge I often wonder how they are able to hide it in plain sight.

"The chemical industry is now the largest manufacturing sector in our nation, a behemoth that grew to revenues of $689 billion in 2008 from $484 billion a year in 2004 and from a relatively modest $2 billion a year in 1962, when Rachel Carson wrote *Silent Spring*. It might more accurately be called the petrochemical industry, since oil is the base for 90 percent of the chemicals" (Shabecoff & Shabecoff, 2010, 40).

This book also talked about how the Centers for Disease Control and Prevention (CDC) had conducted a large study where it found that "one hundred different substances were found in the bodies of the children" (Shabecoff & Shabecoff, 45). When you think about this critically, you begin to realize that the way to manipulate every Karbon being is to manipulate the world of Karbon itself. What one should realize is that the desire to keep this power in the hands of a few is the reason why they have no problem killing off their own.

The reason why melanin beings have to be first in line in this wave of destruction is because we have the power already residing in us. There is no reason for us to be in labs reverse-engineering Karbon technology in order to become more enlightened. This process can be initiated by belief and by works that will reinforce that belief system.

Because they have always been aware of this phenomenon that resides in us, they never miss an opportunity to employ the acme of skill stated in *The Art of War*: "To subdue the enemy without fighting" (Tzu, fifth century). This means that you force your enemies to be at war with themselves, leaving you only with the responsibility to push them in the grave after they have dug it.

The Blancos take it a step further to ensure that your ignorance of Khemistry remains permanent by capturing your imagination with sports and entertainment, as well as stressing you out, as you are forced to prioritize what bills can be paid because you are immersed in a check-to-check cycle.

I will give a few more examples to prove that if you choose to ignore this science, you do so at your own peril. There is a volatile liquid (volatile in Khemistry means a substance that can easily evaporate at room temperatures) extracted from petroleum or Koal tar. It is used to make synthetic rubber. There were experiments conducted in 1994 to see just what effects, if any, isoprene has on the system. Male mice and rats were exposed to isoprene vapors for six months. The study was conducted to find out if "isoprene produces a carcinogenic response similar to that of 1,3-butadiene after intermediate exposure durations" (Melnick, 1994).

What they found was that hyperplasia (the overgrowth of tissue) would occur. They also found that the sexual organs of these mice were adversely affected. Now the reason why this should be alarming is because this is what your condoms are made of. Of course, I'm not suggesting that people ditch condoms and just have unprotected sex, but what I am saying is that when an evil force takes over Nature's system and replaces it with an artificial matrix, every area of activity is at the mercy of those in power. With population control in mind, what better way to control births, than adulterating the most popular tool for birth control?

They also were aware that this Khemical attacks melanin! Rubber has the potential to initiate the onset of vitiligo. Is there any way to trust this was not the plan from a people who propagate to the world, and especially to us, that our skin is a curse and not a gift from the Most High?

In the late eighteenth century, there was a Black guy by the name of Henry Moss who was nicknamed the "Great Curiosity" because at the age of thirty-eight, his skin began a process of depigmentation until he was as fair as the late Michael Jackson. He toured the country showing off his peculiarity to White audiences as they gazed, poked, and prodded, wondering how he "cured" himself of his Blackness. George Washington even paid him a visit to see what all the fuss was about, ironically enough paying a quarter to see the "Great Curiosity."

With the Hamitic curse being pushed by "Christians," and the inferiority complex being pushed by science, the melanin being would be plagued by these stigmas all the way up to the present day. We also know that isoprene is used in skin-lightening creams, which further proves that this campaign to encourage self-hate inside of the melanin being is by design, with the eventuality often accompanied by deadly consequences.

Melanin beings go through hell now just to make it to this realm, and then when we get here, it seems we are placed in a field full of landmines as soon as they cut the umbilical cord. They make sure, at an early age, they make us feel insecure about our gift, until we start a diabolical war within ourselves, as the Blancos wait patiently to push us in the grave we had been digging for an entire lifetime. They have become so successful at this strategy that our own people begin to play critical roles in our voluntary enslavement, although we know this has been the case all throughout history.

In the 1940s, two Black psychologists named Kenneth and Mamie Clark conducted "the doll tests" on Black children and came to the conclusion that Black children could never receive an adequate education when only surrounded by Black faces; they had to be around the Blanco children in order to feel good about themselves. They came to this conclusion because the Black children in the experiment associated bad with the Black dolls and good with the White ones. This experiment is what led to the decision in the Brown v. Board of Education Supreme Court case (LDF, no date).

So, in Black history month, all the Blancos do is praise Thurgood Marshall and yet never tell the truth about the impact of this experiment on the outcome so desperately desired by a people who want us to hate what we are. When US President John F. Kennedy said, "We can secure peace only by preparing for war" (Kennedy, 1960), then I must proclaim that we have never had peace, because we have never had time to prepare. Not until now!

I hope you understand that freedom starts off first as a state of mind, and not something you first have to experience to become acquainted with. Many have become more obsessed with their connection with social media than their connection with Mother Nature. You must know these are the last days, beloved. We are dealing with an organism that has chosen to use the science in a way that guarantees loss of life on a massive scale. When you frequent their grocery stores, they make you pay extra if you desire to consume food without their additives and preservatives.

Many of our people don't understand the depth of this deception because they know very little, if anything, about the world of Khemistry. I hear people all the time say, "I only eat organic foods." The problem with that is that technically *all* natural foods are organic because *all* foods contain Karbon. There is literally no food grown on this earth that is free from pesticides, which is an umbrella term encompassing herbicides, rodenticides, fungicides, etc. The difference is really in the amount, and not that they are two distinct groups of food stuffs. So essentially, one is just more processed than the other, designed for more shelf life, and the other has more of Mother Nature in the ingredients.

This is why the government allows these companies to be liberal in the use of these labels because they know the real meaning behind these titles, which serve as marketing ploys rather than information that helps you make better decisions when grocery shopping. There are those of us who will say, "It's all about the money," but the reality of it is, if they know it makes you unhealthy and addicted, exacerbating chronic illnesses and increasing doctor's office visits, then it's bigger than just the money.

The ignorance of this science, which was our true religion as melanin beings, is the root cause of political, social, economic, and environmental instability. When we discussed rubber and its importance to the Blanco industries, many of us still choose to ignore that these beings were fully aware of its negative effects on the melanin molecule. In an article, "Belgium's Heart of Darkness," published in 2012 by *History Today*, author Tim Stanley details the atrocities the melanin beings of the Congo experienced at the hands of the Belgium snakes who supposedly went there to acquire raw materials for the purposes of satisfying the world's demand for rubber.

Again, because we view the world of the past as we see the world today, it is easy for us to read these articles and miss out on the clues given that will highlight the real reasons as to why these people were over there to begin with. First, we must put things into perspective. Blancos, past and present, have always been in the minority, numerically, in terms of global numbers, so this idea that the "world" had a demand for rubber is just an excuse for the invasion of melanin territories, not to mention, if we had a demand for it and it was sitting on our land, why would we not be involved in mass producing it?

As the article states, Leopold convinced the European powers to give him access to the Congo Basin because he vowed "to bring civilisation to the so-called dark continent" (Stanley, 2012). Imagine, if you will, a people who had no resources of their own, hardly bathed, had no known language until the ninth century, boasting about bringing civilization to Africa. It is noteworthy that

Leopold finds himself in a country "76 times the size of Belgium" (Stanley, 2012).

As I have already proven, the main reason for Leopold undertaking such a huge task was not to bring civilization to the Africans or to even satisfy the demand for rubber for industrial applications, it was because they knew that isoprene attacked melanin! Once they had figured out this "Khemistry," they would do anything to get their hands on it! For those who are still in disbelief, the article goes on to say,

> "Congolese workers were sent out into the jungle to slash down vines and layer their bodies with rubber latex. Later they would scrape it off their skin— often taking flesh and hair with it . . . Villages were set quotas of rubber" (Stanley, 2012).

Because we know this was the process by which they would acquire the rubber, and because we know that millions of these melanin beings died in an effort to complete this labor-intensive task, what conclusion can any sane and rational mind come to? Why do you think, even today, the cosmetic industry is not regulated by the FDA? They are fully aware of the harmful, if not deadly, effects of skin-lightening cream, but it is still allowed to be sold. On the other hand, it's illegal for tanning salons in most states to allow any Blancos under the age of eighteen to frequent those businesses, because they are fully aware of their genetic differences.

This is also the main reason why condoms that are promoted for melanin men were a lot thicker than condoms used by Blancos, and I'm sure they were created with a lot more Khemical volatility than for those used by our counterparts. This is the reason why we should be on guard and realize the real reason as to why they want us to be ignorant of the science of Khemit, or the religion of our people.

When we are ignorant of Khemistry, then we are ignorant of how dark, insidious, and savage the Blancos really are. You cannot help but come to the realization that the end game is inevitable, and there will be no reconciling of differences with those in power. There are those in the so-called conscious community who now have been convinced that the abandonment of the "critical race theory" would be counterproductive in our pursuit to garner clarity on racial issues so we can move past contemporary restraints. Although this "social science" may mean well, it pales in comparison to the progress that can be achieved when melanin beings understand their position as it relates to their role in the world of Khemistry. We, as melanin beings, wonder why Blancos refuse to entertain or endorse certain worldviews and belief systems, and it is because they understand that "the first one to the mind is the winner" (Kamblon, no date).

The first battle takes place in the mind! This is the reason why you will see the full weight of the machine levied against you when you challenge popular narratives disseminated by the status quo. We, as melanin beings, always center on the physical aspect of this tragedy and ignore how important the wars in the mind are.

- How many of us have died prematurely because of "lack of knowledge"?
- How many family members and how many of us suffer daily because our bodies are at war with us?
- How many of our family members are on drugs concocted by Big Pharma, and they have been told they would have to be on for the rest of their lives? It is this ignorance of the world of Khemistry that has led to this eventuality.
- How can the field of health move forward if the Blanco philosophy is to treat disease with disease?

Take herpes, for instance. Most people are unaware that they actually have to test to make sure that it is not a fungal infection versus a "viral" infection, but I digress. The point is that the most popular treatment for this "viral" infection is called acyclovir. The problem is that acyclovir is a synthetic version of guanine. I hope you are wondering what guanine is, because guanine comes from the Spanish word *guano*, which is *bat poop*! So, they are literally treating people's herpes infections with bat poop! This is just one of many examples that proves that the ignorance of Khemistry has led us down a path of ignorance so deep, that when we reach the surface, we still find ourselves at the bottom of its ocean.

Think about this, if what the Blancos have stolen from you makes you think that they are gods, then if these gifts were still in your possession, what would they think of you? I will tell you what they would think of you, they would think of you as the real Superman and the real Superwoman!

Were you aware, according to the "Table," krypton is a real element! Its number is thirty-six, the real three sixes, and you must know as well that krypton just means *hidden*. I am fairly sure that most of you thought these movies were just a product of the imagination of the Blancos because you have given these men and women godlike qualities. Before I go deep into the symbolism of these movies, which gives you the real knowledge of who you are, I will give you an example that will prove that this is their most popular method they use to hide the arcane in plain sight.

If you have children, or if you were a child when this movie came out, you may remember how popular this movie was and its success at the box office, generating almost a billion dollars. It was the highest-grossing animated film at that time, and the second-highest grossing film in 2003. All the way up to 2006, it was the highest-selling DVD, passed up by *Toy Story 3*. It was produced by Pixar Animation Studios and released by Walt Disney Pictures (Wikipedia, no date).

So, the point is, *Finding Nemo* was a huge film, but with as many people who watched the film, none were aware of its symbolism. Now, I am not here to say whether or not Disney is a company that ruins its child stars and oversexualizes them when they come of age; that should already be apparent to you if you have eyes. What I am here to do is to show you how important it is to be in the *know,* so that you are not unwilling participants in their rituals.

The fish that they decided to use for this movie as the main characters are known as clownfish. Well, the peculiar thing about clownfish is that if the "female" fish happens to die, the strongest male will evolve into a female and then mate with the male next in line so as to ensure the survival of the species. Yes, you read that correctly. Nemo needed to be found, because it was an issue of survival, and gradually the "father," which just happened to be the strongest male left in that situation, would have evolved into a "female," so that he and Nemo could ensure the survival of the family for generations to come.

We know pedophilia to be a huge problem, not only within Hollywood but within society as a whole, because when the culture is built on perverse and wayward behavior, extensions from its foundation are merely reflections of its authority. So, it is not so much as Hollywood as it is the system itself. The real question is, how can you get these monsters to stop kidnapping and molesting children, when animals are not even safe?

In ten states, bestiality is still legal, and you must remember the other states had to go through the process of making it illegal, as it was a common practice among the people who came here with the "Founding Fathers."

It is still legal in Washington, DC, which explains why this country is run like a zoo, and even more evidence as to why you should know that you are living in the belly of the beast! Some manner of speech is not figurative in Nature.

So now that you are aware of the importance of symbolism, we must take a deeper look at this Superman character and the symbols present, which are intended to show the nature of the eumelanin and pheomelanin beings. We should know first that most of these characters' attributes (Superman and Superwoman) are qualities inherent of the eumelanin species. The most popular of these being the connection to the Sun. Superman and Superwoman literally receive their power from the Sun!

We fail to realize that the expression of this superhero's abilities is nothing more than the cosmic expressions emanating from the electromagnetic spectrum coming from the Sun. So, the question that should be asked is, "How can a people create a superhero that they will only cast Blanco men for, whose superpowers rely on the Sun, especially considering that they have a hard time being in the Sun?" To expound even further, the nickname of the character they call Superman is the "Man of Steel." This is not a mistake or a name that was given that just sounds good. The reason for this nickname is rooted in the knowledge of Khemistry, which is nothing more than the knowledge of the Karbon realm and the people chosen to protect it.

So, as stated, when we are familiar with the way Karbon works, we know that there is no such thing as any part of his image, or any part of his abilities, that has been put together randomly or by chance. You should know that in order to make steel, you need two forms of energy that the melanin being is already in possession of and given at birth. The first of course is Karbon, and the second is iron. So, in order to make steel, you must bond Karbon and iron together. This is extremely important for you to commit to memory, because melanin beings have Karbon in their skin and iron in their blood, making the Black man and the Black woman the *real* man and woman of steel! This is why they chose the element krypton in order to represent the Superman character, because this is the information that they intended to always remain hidden from the people who have not been chosen by opinion but have been elected by Nature!

Why would the Most High not give you access to these powers when the animals already express them themselves? How can you deny that these powers exist when animals can see for miles, locate prey in the dark, run sixty miles an hour, and spin webs made of material they now make bulletproof vests out of? Why would the Most High give you dominion over a realm and tell you that you are his greatest creation, but yet make you weaker than the ants that forage food for the winter?

These beings were placed here as examples, specifically for a time like this where melanin beings would be in a state of extreme ignorance of what and who they really are. Remember, when you do not know *what* you are, *who* you are can be defined for you. We are the "crystallogens," a group of beings who at the elemental level only bond in crystal formation. We are literally diamonds in human form! Why do you think Blancos commemorate their unions with a diamond! That is what bonds them, the commitment to create even more of these beings who will remain dedicated to the extermination of the vanguards of this realm.

Once again, we find ourselves participating in this ritual because we are unaware of the true religion of the chosen class of people. This diamond form allows us to harness the Sun's energy and manifest endless arrays of beauty and splendor, which bring meaning to the human experience. Look at the culture you have brought to the world when you thought you were slaves. *Imagine* what you can bring to the world when you think you are gods. Remember the Blanco beginnings and Nature as well, so you understand how to navigate through this evil terrain.

Those who are adept know that the original "Greeks" were Black, and that the original "Greeks" did not go by this name. If we are to look at this story through the lens of Nature, we would have no problem drawing this conclusion. In Athens, during the summer, temperatures can exceed 100 degrees! Not to mention that the southern part of Greece is *subtropical*! Now I ask you, considering that the highest rates of skin cancer are in regions where Blancos choose to inhabit, even at a time where they have access to sunscreen and modern technology, how do you think they would have fared, thousands of years ago? On a side note, it is ironic that the only place in Europe that can grow cotton is Greece.

Recall, as well, that as there is no debate, we are the oldest people on the so-called planet, there is certainly no debate we have the oldest languages on this so-called planet as well. The Coptic language is written in the Greek alphabet with the exception of seven letters, and this was the very language used to decode the Rosetta Stone, which in turn was used to decipher the hieroglyphs! Because we know, according to Nature, that Egypt was in a region that literally gave fair-skinned individuals cancer, and that the way Egyptians and Greeks dressed left the majority of their bodies exposed to the Sun, I will ask you, who do you think the Egyptians and Greeks were?

See, Blancos have made you poor and inept for a reason, how many of us have been out of our own state, let alone out of the country? We often forget, before virtual reality and living vicariously through the internet was a thing, books were responsible for this experience. If you even look at it from the standpoint of cultural transmission, from the Greeks to the Romans, they even speak of a time where this transition is known as the Greco-Roman empire. This is a period of time when the number of Blancos started to increase, and as it proves all throughout human history, the more their numbers increased, the more power you see taken away from melanin beings.

This was a period of time dominated by amalgamation,

or the mixing of races. It's no different than any other time when Blancos went to a land dominated by people of color. It's just that because a lot of our people see them as gods and conquerors, we view rape as an expression of dominance and not one of necessity. That's why mixed races are given the consideration and power over darker-skinned individuals because they are literally the bridge used to keep the gap between us and them, as well as successfully steal the legacy from the chosen class. The 2002 movie *Rabbit-Proof Fence,* which is based on true events, proves this without a shadow of a doubt, telling the story of how mixed-race girls were sent to a training camp to integrate them into White society.

Even if we were to take a look at the origins of these two nations, Greece and Rome, and analyze the myths, they still lead you to draw the same conclusion. The beginning of Greece is said to have started after a flood that Zeus caused in order to cleanse humanity. Prometheus's son, Deucalion, and his wife, Pyrrha, were chosen to be the survivors, and Deucalion was told to build an ark by Zeus so that he and his family would survive the flood. Does this sound familiar to you? Most Bibles say that these are the "Greek scriptures" and that should have made you think twice anyway, but I digress.

They had at least two children and one of those children was named Hellen, the mother of Greece. This is why they refer to any period involving Greece as the Hellenistic period. The question that should be asked here is, "If 'social scientists' and historians refer to Greece as the Hellenistic period and Hellen was supposed to be a myth, why do they teach it as if she really existed?" The reason is simple, and I have stated this time and time again, it is because science merely picks up where religion left off!

The point is, just like the Egyptians, the people have their beginnings rooted in the lineage of the gods, but this is not the same when we look at the Romans. The story goes that the princess, Rhea Silvia, who was the daughter of Numitor, king of Alba Longa, had two twin boys fathered by the god Mars, the god of *war*, and their names were Romulus and Remus. Their evil uncle snatched power away from the king and because of this, Rhea was in fear for the lives of the boys and sent them sailing down the Tiber River. The boys were then found by Capitoline, the she-wolf or Lupa Capitolina, and they suckled on this wolf until they were found by a shepherd named Faustulus who then took them home and raised them.

When the boys got older, Romulus killed his twin brother and named the place where they were found after himself, and thus the city of Rome was born. Blancos often debate about why Romulus killed his own brother, but when your father is the god of war, what do you expect?

Now, having some idea of their beginnings, why does it surprise us that the Blancos have so much love for the canine, which is bred from the wolf? Remember the name of the wolf that found them was named Capitoline, which is not too far off from "capital," which identifies the central city of each state. They may have changed the spelling, but they made sure it sounds the same, because, as stated before, the world is ruled by signs and symbols.

What's even more fascinating is when you go even deeper. The "storming of the US Capitol" on January 6, 2021, was symbolic of the Blancos returning to their wolf-like nature. The obsession with Mars should not be too hard to figure out as well.

So, now that you have a greater understanding of both of our nature, can you not see why they say the world is ruled by signs and symbols? So, when we go back and look at the "Man of Steel" and who it actually represents, we often forget it was symbolic of a time when the Blancos began to make strides in industry, most notably the one they called the "Industrial Revolution." They literally went steel crazy! The buildings got huge, and they called them skyscrapers, symbolic of saying that they could get close to the Sun. Because what most do not realize and have not put together, is that these buildings would allow them to be out in the daylight longer, avoiding the burns associated with prolonged Sun exposure, because Karbon bonds with Karbon, or in other words, Karbon absorbs the Sun's rays!

Once again, people with melanin began to associate this with prowess and genius and not with an issue of survival and necessity. Did you think Buckingham Palace in London, England, was huge because it showcased the greatness of royalty, or because it showed the limitations of this species in that they needed protection from the Sun? Hopefully, you chose the latter, understanding that only big buildings and higher latitudes could accomplish such a feat.

You see, when you use Nature to answer some of life's most perplexing questions, it's short and sweet, yet when you argue your point based on the information given to you by the matrix, you have to write books as thick as encyclopedias. With Nature, the symbols become vivid and begin to speak to you without any need for an expert to interpret.

Look at the symbol on the chest of Superman, is that not in the shape of a diamond? Look at the colors used to represent his costume. When these colors are mixed, do they not make the color purple, which is the color of royalty? Also, his greatest weakness is represented by the color green, which is the color of Mother Nature.

So, in essence through this character, he decides to show his weakness as well. The Blancos are a carnivore/wolf energy and the Karbon baby is literally plant energy. This is why the Blancos have so much disdain for Mother Nature and will overfish her oceans, dump nuclear waste in her streams, chop down her trees, hunt down her wildlife, and block out her Sun! If they were the real Supermen and Superwomen, why would they block out the Sun? Is not that the power source of this superhero?

When the movie *Batman v Superman: Dawn of Justice* was released in 2016, no one put two and two together. You have a man who lives in a cave, gets all his power from AI technology, and then you have a man whose power comes from the Sun and is impervious to everything, except some made-up weakness, which actually is symbolic of the Blanco weakness.

Batman is symbolic of a group of people who are a vector species, carriers of numerous pathogens, specifically rabies. The bat is the quintessence of a virulent species, and the only way you can test for rabies in a bat is if you take out the brain. Why do you think he makes a million Batman and vampire movies, whose symbol just so happens to be the bat?

We must remember that bats are mammals, and bats and birds are in two distinct categories. Bats produce live young and milk for their babies, while birds lay eggs. But the one thing they both have in common is how toxic their poop is. Their droppings are loaded with fungus, that when inhaled can cause histoplasmosis, which is when the fungus invades the lungs and could cause those organs to shut down. This is why they use bat poop to fight off "herpes," because, remember, they use disease to fight disease.

With as much turmoil, confusion, and disorder that Mother Nature and her chosen class have had to suffer through, we tend to chalk it up to random, aimless, or arbitrary behavior on the part of the Blancos, but there is a method to the madness, and the end will always justify the means.

Take, for instance, the slaughtering of the buffalo, which is a misnomer for the American wild bison. The numbers, at their peak, were probably close to forty million, then in the late-nineteenth century, they virtually exterminated the herds and their grazing lands and replaced them with cattle ranches. To an individual who is not familiar with Khemistry, they will assume this was just another classic case of the Blancos displaying destructive behavior, but to the individual who is familiar with alkhemy, they unravel an enigma that is much more sinister.

"Previously, it was thought that natural selection favoured milk drinkers only in more northern regions because of their greater need for vitamin D in their diet. People living in most parts of the world make vitamin D when sunlight hits the skin, but in northern latitudes there isn't enough sunlight to do this for most of the year" (University College London, 2009).

The article goes on further to state,

"Germanic and Celtic people practiced cattle dairying and drank fresh milk in significant amounts . . . The spread of fresh milk drinking from the Balkans across Europe also explains why most European lactase-persistent people carry the same version of the gene; it surfed on a wave of population expansion that followed the rapid co-evolution of milk tolerance and dairy farming" (University College London, 2009).

The reason why this is extremely important to know is because lactose is a sugar made by two simple sugars, glucose and galactose! These two sugars come together to make the sugar lactose to feed the Karbon baby, and because the Blanco woman was not producing the sugar necessary for her children's survival, they needed the cow to help with this, as well as supplying the body with enough vitamin D, not just because there was not a lot of Sun in higher latitudes, but because even if they were able to receive more Sun exposure, because of their fair skin they would have risked acquiring skin cancer! Notice too how the article says "People living in most parts of the world make vitamin D when sunlight hits the skin," as if they do not know who these people are!

Now you know the reason why the buffalo numbers were dramatically reduced, and also why Blanco women would have melanin women breastfeed their babies! Once again, because you look at the Blancos' behavior as an expression of dominance and not one of necessity, and because you are ignorant of Khemistry, all of this escapes your awareness.

Notice as well that it spoke of the Germanic people, who most are unaware that the English are a Germanic tribe! Any linguist will tell you that language branches are related genetically. The Germanic branch of the Indo-European language consists of English, Dutch, and German! So, when the Blancos make movies about the Germans and Hitler and act like they are not related to them, or are of a completely different stock, it shows you how deep this rabbit hole really goes.

So, in conclusion, this German tribe, which was just as vicious as any other German sect, needed the sugar in the milk to feed their young, which also led to the wholesale murder of the Karbon species you refer to as the buffalo, replacing them with the cow in order to ensure their survival. As always, they turn their weaknesses into strengths by romanticizing that era by making films about "cowboys and Indians," and because you see this as a display of dominance, you think this is nothing more than a story of "how the West was won."

The last and final question you should ask yourself is, "Has this manuscript just been written to overload the brain with what has been hidden in plain sight without any hope or resolutions?" I really do hope that what you have learned so far would prevent you from drawing such an immature and fearful response. How long will you sit by, doubting the power of the eumelanin molecule while the Blancos sit in their labs and stretch the limits of their imagination? While you remain in a state of disbelief and arrested development, they are turning sci-fi movies into reality!

If none of these things were possible or true, why would animals be capable of such feats, and technology be evolving at lightspeeds?! You must know that not only does our livelihood depend on this central power source, but the inventions that compel us to describe this satanic world as technologically advanced comes from this central source as well. The electromagnetic spectrum is emitted from the Sun, in the order from least to greatest, there are radio waves, microwaves, infrared, visible, ultraviolet, X-rays, and gamma rays, which are all different manifestations of the same phenomena!

This spectrum is a range of frequencies of electromagnetic *radiation,* which is responsible for the technology that makes life so advanced. Radio waves, as you have guessed, give you your radio. Microwaves allow you to heat food in minutes, while also allowing you to talk on cell phones. Visible light allows you to see your way through this realm, as X-rays allow you to see through the human body! All this wonder and magnificence is emitted by the Sun, and you continue to believe only what you can see, while the Blancos continue to create with what you cannot.

Imagine going back in time a couple of hundred years and you were told to explain to someone how a cell phone or the internet works. Would you not seem as crazy as you may think I am right now as I try to explain to you how the godlike molecule works? Let us not be in a state of disbelief, waiting too late to take advantage of our abilities, as the curtains draw to a close. As Blancos entertain measures to bring about high levels of transhumanism, we will be stuck engaging in debates and protests trying to convince the elite why they should consider us as equals.

When they transcend human limitations, which is already a reality, how well will these arguments and childish posturing serve you? If it appears that I am from 200 years in the future to come back and tell you how melanin works, then let me be the outcast who holds on to the beauty of Khemit while fending off the backlash from the ignorant. Because we have provided overwhelming evidence that the Blancos have used "science" to justify the subjugation of the chosen class, that they have used disease to treat disease, and that their "advanced technology" is nothing more than the manipulation of the electromagnetic spectrum and the reverse-engineering of Nature's wildlife.

This evidence tends to highlight the parasitical nature of this group of people rather than bolstering the identities of innovators and trailblazers, I think it is safe to say without any doubts that there *is no such thing as a Blanco scientist*! Now that we know that the "science" that spills forth from the matrix is pure fallacy, let us hear from the one of those who grew from the seed of the Karbon baby. Nur Ankh Amen gives us more of an accurate description of what this godlike molecule is capable of. Amen echoes the sentiments of Nature in terms of what the Most High knew would serve best for function and greater accessibility to higher levels of awareness, stating,

"Melanocytes are neuron-like cells which produce melanin and numerous proteins in response to electromagnetic radiation . . . You may be asking yourself why the Europeans did not use the Ankh for its intended purpose, or how could an object be virtually ignored in Europe. This is because the Europeans lacked melanin which is an organic semiconductor, that acts as a detector (sixth sense). Without an electric skin, an ankh is practically useless" (Amen, 2001).

These weapons that we were wielding in the past were tied to our vessel, our essence, or the godlike molecule we know as melanin. There was no need for advances in the field of electromagnetism, because we were and still are the technology! Energy is *everywhere*! The idea that energy is scarce and only controlled by the elite is the sole reason people fear the breakdown of society.

We have already spoken about the melanin king named Moses who invented an atmospheric water machine providing hundreds of thousands of gallons of water a day to our melanin brothers and sisters in Flint, Michigan. But where were the mainstream media or even the Black conscious community concerning this amazing feat! This machine literally snatches water out of the air, giving people access to an unlimited supply of fresh water, yet the Blancos' narrative is more popular and more controversial, bombarding you with news of wells, lakes, and aquifers drying up, promoting scarcity that cements in the mind of the layperson the inevitability of societal collapse.

They can incite panic by telling the public which resource in short supply, or the grocery stores being in danger of shutting down, as if the ground can no longer grow food, and people can't raise chickens and cows on their own (if that is the diet you choose to entertain, but you get the point). There is enough electrical power in the air in your bedroom to power a neighborhood, yet you still have a childlike interpretation of what energy is and where it comes from.

You sit back and imagine the world being like the *Jetsons* or *Star Trek,* forty to fifty years from now, not because of what you plan to accomplish, but because you wait to see what Blancos will introduce to humanity. I should say from experience that logic dictates, whatever it is they come out with, it will be to enslave and not to serve humanity.

Most of all, the Most High has given you dreams to make sure that you always reconnect to the spiritual realm, where *everything is possible*! How many dreams have you had where you could fly or hear and see things that would be considered impossible in this "reality"? The spiritual realm is there not because it just complements the physical experience, it's literally where this "reality" is birthed from! This is why when Karbon babies are born they spend more time sleeping than time in this "reality." This is literally the reason for their growth in this realm! Imagine denying your infant sleep for the first three years of its life and expecting the child to remain healthy?

This is also the time in a child's life where their brain makes the most connections in the brain! Even as adults, we can only remain in this realm for so long before we must sleep to regain the "real" energy it takes to remain in this realm. It does not matter how healthy you eat, if you do not get the sleep needed to rejuvenate the vessel! How many have dreamed of a loved one and the next day run into them or received a call from them? The "dream world" helps you to finetune the body.

When you were young, you had to learn to stop wetting the bed. This is a job you accomplished while you were asleep, *not awake*! The problem is, we stop prematurely and refuse to finetune *every organ* in the body while our imagination is at full strength. Even our sexual energy is finetuned while we are inside of this spiritual realm. Even before many people have ever had a sexual experience, they have one in the spiritual realm.

"Science" calls these experience "nocturnal emissions," or you know them better as wet dreams. Your mind, in conjunction with the spiritual realm, recreates reality perfectly! Most people pay attention to the people they know who may be in the dream, and the cosmos recreates the whole experience, from the streets, to the cars, to the buildings, to the time of day, and even whether you or the people you interact with are young or old! This is how creative the superconscious is, yet the conscious mind might not be able to even draw a stick figure!

How many people say they are bad at math, yet the superconscious keeps tracks of *billions* of cells twenty-four hours a day! When you can bring that mind into this "reality," then you have achieved the highest level of enlightenment! You literally spend almost half of your life in this realm, yet when most people write an autobiography, they never mention one dream! That you are even "dreaming" is mind-boggling, considering that you are manufacturing light, all while your eyes are *closed*!

If this is not the realm of the Most High, then why would she use this realm to communicate with the patriarchs in the Bible? Aside from dreams, how many have had déjà vu and still refuse to believe that "time" may not be fixed? We experience some, if not all of these, things and yet we choose to ignore them. How long will we deny our greatness, arresting our development, while they accelerate in speed and growth in the realm of transhumanism?

Do you think that in order to confront the issues facing your people, you can use the same mind that was used to ensure your fall from grace? This is the season of enlightenment, and absolutely nothing can stop a determined spirit whose soul is drenched in melanin! I proclaim to you from the highest mountain, known as the "crown chakra," that many lands have been conquered, many seas have been crossed, searching for the secret that would bridge the divine to the mundane.

Many lives have been sacrificed and many wounds have not healed as the elite have mastered how to turn blood into wine. How many families have been broken in this hell, shedding so many tears that the devil doesn't have to pray for rain? I'm here to tell you, it doesn't matter how many songs you sing or poems you recite, there is no greater masterpiece than melanin, which means no matter how many legends are told from libraries burned to the ground, there will never be a greater story told, than the untold story of the Karbon baby.

REFERENCES

Amen, Nur Ankh. *The Ankh: African Origin of Electromagnetism.* EWorld Inc. 2001.

American Cancer Society. "Early History of Cancer." See https://www.cancer.org/cancer/cancer-basics/history-of-cancer/what-is-cancer.html#written_by.

BBC News. "Diamond Star Thrills Astronomer." February 16, 2004. See http://news.bbc.co.uk/2/hi/3492919.stm.

The Conversation. "Women of Color Spend More than $8 Billion on Bleaching Creams Worldwide Every Year." February 19, 2021. See https://theconversation.com/women-of-color-spend-more-than-8-billion-on-bleaching-creams-world-wide-every-year-153178.

Creamer, John. "Poverty Rates for Blacks and Hispanics Reached Historic Lows in 2019." United States Census Bureau. September 15, 2020. See https://www.census.gov/library/stories/2020/09/poverty-rates-for-blacks-and-hispanics-reached-historic-lows-in-2019.html.

Diamond, Jared. *Guns, Germs, and Steel: The Fates of Human Societies.* W.W. Norton. 1999.

Dillin, John. "More Blacks Enter Middle Class, But Poverty Lingers, Study Says." *The Christian Science Monitor.* August 9, 1991. See https://www.csmonitor.com/1991/0809/09071.html.

Ebony Mag Team. "Cheers! Craft Beers Brewed by African American Gaining Popularity." *Blavity.* October 17, 2015. See https://blavity.com/cheers-craft-beers-brewed-by-african-americans-gaining-popularity?category1=21ninety-food&category2=cooking.

Faragher, John Mack, general editor. *The American Heritage Encyclopedia of American History.* Henry Holt and Co. 1998.

Gallagher, James. "Drug That Creates a 'Real Sun-Tan' Could Prevent Cancer." *BBC News.* June 13, 2017. See https://www.bbc.com/news/health-40260029.

Green, Dan S., and Earl Smith. "W.E.B. Dubois and the Concepts of Race and Class." *Phylon* 44:4 (1983): 262–272. doi:10.2307/274576.

India Today Web Desk. "When and Why Did the British First Choose to Invade India?" *India Today.* August 26, 2019. See https://www.indiatoday.in/education-today/gk-current-affairs/story/when-and-why-british-first-came-to-india-1591166-2019-08-24.

Jablonski, Nina G. *Skin: A Natural History.* University of California Press. 2006.

Jefferson, Thomas. Letter to William Stephens Smith. November 13, 1787. See https://www.snopes.com/fact-check/thomas-jefferson-tree-of-liberty/.

Kambon, Obadele. "Forum." KMTYW Social Education Communiversity. See https://www.abibitumi.com/community/photos-and-videos/dr-obadele-kambon-he-nana-akufo-addos-plan-to-make-french-compulsory/.

Kennedy, John F. Speech at the Civic Auditorium. Seattle, Washington. September 6, 1960. See www.presidency.ucsb.edu.

Klug, Aaron. "Francis Crick (8 June 1916–28 July 2004): A Memoir." *FEBS Letters* 579: 4 (February 7, 2005): 852–854. See https://febs.onlinelibrary.wiley.com/doi/full/10.1016/j.febslet.2004.10.103.

Kochhar, Rajesh. "Shipbuilding in India: Wadia Shipbuilders." In *Encyclopaedia of the History of Science, Technology, and Medicine in Non-Western Cultures.* Helaine Selin, editor. Springer. 2008.

Landis, John, director. *Coming to America.* Paramount Pictures. 1988.

Las Casas, Bartolomé De. *A Short Account of the Destruction of the Indies*. Penguin. 2004.

LDF (NAACP Legal Defense and Educational Fund, Inc.). "A Revealing Experiment: Brown v. Board and "The Doll Test." See https://www.naacpldf. org/ldf-celebrates-60th-anniversary-brown-v-board-education/ significance-doll-test/.

Leverett, Thomas. "How the Sun Sees You." August 12, 2014. See https://www.youtube.com/watch?v=o9BqrSAHbTc.

Lipton, Bruce H. *The Biology of Belief: Unleashing the Power of Consciousness, Matter, and Miracles*. Hay House. 2008.

Melnick, Ronald L. *NTP Technical Report on Toxicity Studies of Isoprene*. National Institutes of Health Publication 94-3354. US Department of Health and Human Services. July 1994.

Money, Nicholas P. *The Rise of Yeast: How the Sugar Fungus Shaped Civilization*. Oxford University Press. 2018.

Moss, Michael. *Salt Sugar Fat: How the Food Giants Hooked Us*. Random House. 2013.

New York Times. "Mark Twain Is Dead at 74." (April 22, 1910). See https://www.nytimes.com/1910/04/22/archives/mark-twain-is-dead-at-74-end-comes-peacefully-at-his-new-england.html.

O'Dell, Larry. "All-Black Towns." *Oklahoma Historical Society*. See https://www.okhistory.org/publications/enc/entry.php?entry=AL009.

Okpokwasili, G.C., and C.N. Molokwu. "Yeast and Mould Contaminants of Vegetable Oils." *Bioresource Technology* 57:3 (September 1996), 245–249.

Schaefer, Anna. "Is Gatorade Bad for You?" *Healthline*. October 2, 2018. See https://www.healthline.com/health/ food-nutrition/is-gatorade-bad-for-you.

Shabecoff, Philip, and Alice Shabecoff. *Poisoned Profits: The Toxic Assault on Our Children.* Random House. 2010.

Skin Cancer Foundation. "Skin Cancer Facts & Statistics: What You Need to Know." See https://www.skincancer.org/skin-cancer-information/skin-cancer-facts/.

Stanley, Tim. "Belgium's Heart of Darkness." *History Today* 62:10 (October 2012). See https://www.historytoday.com/archive/contrarian/belgiums-heart-darkness.

Tanzilo, Bobby. "Peoples Was America's among First Black-Owned Breweries." *OnMilwaukee.* February 6, 2016. See https://onmilwaukee.com/articles/peoples.

Thompson, Larry. "Science under Fire behind the Clash between Congress and Nobel Laureate David Baltimore." *The Washington Post.* (May 9, 1989). See https://www.washingtonpost.com/archive/lifestyle/wellness/1989/05/09/science-under-fire-behind-the-clash-between-congress-and-nobel-laureate-david-baltimore/3068efef-b614-4a89-84f8-6ac721f5d187/.

Thornton, Mark. "Alcohol Prohibition Was a Failure." *Cato Institute.* July 17, 1991. See https://www.cato.org/policy-analysis/alcohol-prohibition-was-failure.

Twain, Mark. *Following the Equator: A Journey around the World, Volume 2.* Harper and Brothers. 1890.

Tzu, Sun. *The Art of War.* Fifth century. See https://www.google.com/books/edition/The_Art_of_War/QhsZEAAAQBAJ?hl=en&gbpv=0.

University College London. "Milk Drinking Started around 7,500 Years Ago in Central Europe." *ScienceDaily.* September 1, 2009. See www.sciencedaily.com/releases/2009/08/090827202513.htm.

Waterman, Morgan. "Race, Segregation, and Incarceration in the States, 1920–2010." *History 90.01: Topics in Digital History.* October 31, 2016. See https://journeys.dartmouth.edu/censushistory/2016/10/31/

rough-draft-race-segregation-and-incarceration-in-the-states-1920-2010/.

Wikipedia. *Finding Nemo*. Pixar Animation Studios. 2003. See https://en.wikipedia.org/wiki/Finding_Nemo.

ACKNOWLEDGMENTS

Thank you to Joni and Deborah for helping to bring a jewel from the dream world into this reality. Also thanks to the F.O.F squad and all the support and positive energy you sent on my Youtube channel; Phoenix Windwalker who motivated me to stay on course; Kafiahmad who was able to get the cover done in a timely fashion without compromising creativity; my haters who gave me the hunger and drive to succeed; and last but definitely not least, the Most High who makes every and ALL things possible . . . so even if I succeed in life . . . if I do not gain the Most High's approval . . . I have failed in everything . . . and if you have read this book in its entirety, may you now walk in the new light that shines forth from the Karbon Baby."